A Practical Step-by-Step Guide to

INDOOR
GARDENING

A Practical Step-by-Step Guide to

INDOOR
GARDENING

WHITECAP BOOKS

5084
This edition published in 1998 by Whitecap Books Ltd., 351 Lynn Avenue
North Vancouver, B.C., Canada V7J 2C4
© 1998 CLB International
A division of Quadrillion Publishing Ltd,
Godalming, Surrey, GU7 1XW, England.
Printed and bound in Singapore.
ISBN 1-55110-707-4

Credits
Compiled and typeset by: Ideas into Print
Photographs: Neil Sutherland
Production: Neil Randles, Karen Staff

THE PHOTOGRAPHER
Neil Sutherland has more than 25 years experience in a wide range of
photographic fields, including still-life, portraiture, reportage, natural history,
cookery, landscape and travel. His work has been published in countless books
and magazines throughout the world.

Contributors
John Feltwell, Nicholas Hall, Colin Lewis, Sue Phillips, Yvonne Rees,
Wilma Rittershausen, David Squire, Rosemary Titterington.

Half-title page: Clivia miniata *has elegant foliage and striking orange flowers.*
Title page: Dracaena deremensis *'Green Stripe' and a group of African violets.*
Left: *A magnificent display of orchids, ferns and other foliage plants indoors.*
Right: *Juniper is an excellent subject for creating a flowing bonsai shape.*

CONTENTS

Below: The exquisite flowers of Hoya lanceolata *ssp.* bella *hang from trailing stems and have a wonderful fragrance.*

Below: A cluster of stems bearing violet-blue flowers springs from the central rosette of leaves in this fine streptocarpus hybrid.

Above: Basil is worth growing as an annual plant in cooler climates for its flavor. When dried, it has a completely different taste.

PART 3: GARDENING IN THE SUNROOM

CONTENTS

Above: This Japanese maple is the result of many years of training. From a tiny seedling, it has developed into an informal upright subject.

PART 4: ENJOYING BONSAI

PART 5: GROWING ORCHIDS

Below: One of the many hybrids of Miltoniopsis. *The popular pansy orchids are ideal for beginners and good subjects for growing indoors.*

Above: Impatiens *New Guinea Group have dark foliage and masses of flowers in a range of bright colors from spring until the fall.*

PART 6: HOUSEPLANT SELECTION

Part One

GARDENING INDOORS

Selecting and buying, watering and feeding, potting and displaying houseplants are fundamental facets of growing plants indoors. Growing plants in pots indoors or in a sunroom is not as easy as you might think. Outdoors – and when planted in the ground – the yearly cycle of seasons strongly influences growth, and plants are always in harmony with their surroundings. Indoors, however, plants are expected to thrive and create eye-catching displays, although they are often living in conditions that are alien to them. Frequently, there is a wide range of plants in a room, all demanding different temperatures and amounts of light. And although plants can be selected to suit varying amounts of light in a room, they all usually have to survive in the same temperature, which may vary radically during the winter when the heating is turned off at night. In the first part of this book we examine the skills needed to look after houseplants, including what to look for when buying them, how to judge whether they need watering, and how to feed, topdress and repot them. There is guidance on caring for your houseplants while you are away from home, and if despite your best efforts, your houseplants should succumb to attack from pests or disease do not despair; help is at hand in the form of a detailed advice on common houseplant problems and how to tackle them.

Left: Cape primroses flower from spring until fall. **Right:** *A cyclamen brings welcome blooms to the home in winter.*

Selecting and buying houseplants

Choosing and buying plants for the home requires as much care as when buying any other item. Before buying a plant, examine it closely and reject it if the leaves are wilting, which indicates that the potting mixture is either too dry or too wet. If the potting mix is covered in green slime, do not buy the plant. Make sure that there is no evidence of pests or disease on any part of the plant and avoid specimens that are not properly labelled and any that are displayed in cold, drafty positions, as their buds may drop off later. Do not be tempted by low-cost plants with bare stems and few leaves, as they never recover fully. Buying a low-cost plant that dies during the following week makes it an expensive buy.

Above: Avoid houseplants with roots coming out of the drainage holes in their pots. This is a sign that they need repotting. If left for too long in this starved condition, plants seldom recover and will not be attractive.

Above: Moss on pots indicates that the plant has remained too long in its pot and its growth may have been restricted. Although the moss can be removed, the plant may not recover.

Above: Large plants in small pots are deprived of essential nutrients for healthy growth. Small plants in large pots are difficult to water. When roots do not fill most of the pot, the potting mixture often becomes stagnant.

Above: Plants bought while in full bloom – or with faded flowers – only remain attractive for a limited period. Inspect the plant carefully and only buy flowering plants that have plenty of flower buds still to open.

Taking plants home

Houseplants can only succeed if they arrive home safely, and quickly become established in their new environment. Take them home and unwrap them as quickly as possible. Place newly bought plants in moderate warmth, out of direct and strong sunlight. Do not knock flowering plants, as their buds may then fall off. Ensure that the potting mixture is moist but not waterlogged. About a week after bringing a plant home, move it to its permanent position. Do not keep moving it about, especially if it is delicate. Do not worry if a few leaves or buds initially fall off; the plant is probably just settling down.

Above: *Plants that are in a poor state of health when you buy them never recover, irrespective of how much care and attention they are subsequently given. Stems that have lost their leaves never again become properly clothed.*

Above: *Healthy houseplants enrich a home for many months, sometimes years. Damaged plants, as well as those infested with pests and diseases, inevitably engender disappointment. The first step to success with houseplants is to inspect them carefully before buying, and then to get them home safely and quickly.*

17

Pots and potting mixtures

Pots and potting mixture are essential to growing plants indoors. Traditional pots for plants were made of clay, but more recently plastic ones have gained supremacy. However, plants will grow healthily in both types, and both have advantages and disadvantages. Both clay and plastic pots are sold in a range of sizes, from 2in(5cm) to about 15in (38cm) wide. These measurements indicate the distance across the inside at the top of the pot. The depth of a pot is about the same as the width. Small pots increase in 0.5in(1.25cm) stages, larger ones in 1in(2.5cm) or 2in(5cm) increments. Cache pots, also known as cover pots, surround growing pots, creating an attractive feature as well as complementing and highlighting home decor. Most are round, plain or decorated, and available in a wide range of colors. However, some – and especially the larger types – are square, with the largest mounted on casters. Many old home artefacts also make good cache pots. The prime danger with them is that when plants are watered, excess water may remain in the base and eventually cause roots to decay. To avoid this problem, tip away any water in the base of the cache pot about ten minutes after watering a plant. Because pots have holes in the base to allow excess water to drain, stand them on saucers or in cache pots to prevent damaging decorative surfaces. Saucers are available in a range of colors, some matching the growing pot for a coordinated design.

Left: Loam soils are usually used in clay pots (left) and peat types in plastic pots (right). Plants grow just as successfully in both types of pot.

Plastic pots

Plastic pots are are light and easy to handle and available in a wide color range. There is no need to cover the small drainage holes with crocks, and as plastic is not porous, the potting mixture needs less frequent watering. They are usually used in conjunction with peat-based potting mixtures. Plastic pots may become brittle with age, especially if stored outdoors and at low temperatures.

Clay pots

Clay pots are much heavier than plastic ones and therefore create a firm base for large plants. They are a natural color and harmonize with all plants, and their porous nature allows damaging salts to escape from the potting mixture. This is especially important if plants are fed excessively. Clay pots encourage potting mixtures to remain cool in summer and warm in winter. They are usually used in conjunction with loam-based potting mixtures. However, clay pots usually break when dropped and are more difficult to clean than plastic ones. If they are dry, be sure to soak them in water

Right: The pot should be in balance with the size of the plant, as shown here. Avoid large plants in small pots, and small plants in large pots, as it makes watering them very difficult.

Types of potting mixture

Loam-based potting mixtures are formed from sterilized soil, sharp sand and peat, whereas peat-based types are wholly created from peat. Loam-based mixes are heavier than peat types and therefore give greater stability to large plants. They are unlikely to dry out so fast or so completely as peat-based types and have a larger reserve of minor and trace plant foods than peat-based potting mixes.

Peat-based mixes are more uniform than loam-based types (the quality of the loam is frequently variable), are relatively light to carry home and are easy to store. Simply seal the bag and keep it in a dry, cool place. Peat-based mixes are suitable for most plants, but start feeding plants at an earlier stage than with loam-based types. Peat mixes dry out more quickly and are more difficult to remoisten if watering has been neglected.

Garden soil is not suitable for growing plants in pots indoors, as it is variable in quality, often badly drained and may contain weed seeds, pests and diseases. Plants can be grown without any potting mixture at all. This technique is known as hydroculture, also known as hydroponics.

Above: Garden soil   **Below:** Peat-based mixture

Above: Houseplants in garden soil (left) underachieve. Healthy houseplants will grow successfully in both loam-based mixes (center) and peat-based potting mixtures (right).

Right: Loam-based mixture

Light and warmth

Light and warmth, provided outdoors by sunlight, activate the growing process in plants. In the open air, light and warmth are in harmony and balance, the temperature rising with an increase in light intensity. There is also a close relationship between the seasons and light and warmth. However, plants indoors are often expected to thrive in low light and high temperatures. Plants vary enormously in their need for light. As a general rule, flowering plants need more light than those grown for their foliage. Remember that the intensity of light varies seasonally, and plants that thrive on a sunny window in winter may need more shade in summer. However, plants placed close to windows in winter for maximum light, may suffer from cold drafts, causing flower buds to drop off. Bear in mind that light intensity decreases rapidly as the distance from a window increases. For example, at 8ft(2.5m) from a window the light is only 5-10% of that on a windowsill. Full sun, especially in summer, scorches the leaves of most houseplants except cacti and other succulents. Do not move plants suddenly from a dull position into very strong light. Instead, accustom them gradually to better light. Keep windows clean when light intensity is low. In summer, net curtains help to diffuse strong light.

Artificial lighting

'Growing lights' suspended over plants to supplement low light levels are especially useful in winter to keep plants healthy and growing. Suspend the light source 6-12in(15-30cm) above flowering plants and 12-24in (30-60cm) above those primarily grown for their attractive foliage. Use the lights about twelve hours each day. Do not leave them on all night.

Above: *Exposure to strong light is just as harmful as too little light. The leaves of this peperomia have wilted and shriveled. Thick-leaved plants are less affected than thin-leaved types.*

The plant on the right was given slight shade, especially in summer.

Above: *Plants that are deprived of light become unsightly and eventually deteriorate to a point where recovery is impossible. The polkadot plant (Hypoestes phyllostachya) on the left*

was kept in a dark spot, while the one on the right was grown in good light.

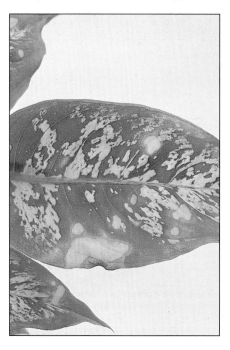

Above: *Leaves form blisters when water droplets fall on them and they are then exposed to strong sunlight. The water acts as a lens, intensifying the light and burning the leaf.*

Above: *Plants naturally grow towards light. To prevent the stems and leaves bending over in an unsightly manner, turn foliage plants, such as this dieffenbachia, a quarter of a turn*

Above: *Temperatures that change rapidly between day and night, and especially during daylight, soon cause leaves to fall off. Potting mix that is too wet or dry also contributes to the fall of leaves. Plants with thicker and tougher leaves, such as the ivy shown above, are not damaged so severely.*

Above: *High temperatures, low humidity and dry potting mix cause plants to wilt and their foliage to shrivel. Leaves become crisp and dry, eventually falling off and creating an unsightly plant. In good conditions, plants retain their glossy leaves, as seen above on this weeping fig.*

every few days. Plants that are turned regularly retain an even outline.

Above: *Low temperatures are just as damaging to plants as high ones. The plant ceases to grow and eventually collapses. The leaves and flowers around the outside are affected first. Getting the temperature right makes a significant difference to a plant's growth. The tuberous begonia shown on the right is a good example of this.*

Watering houseplants

Like all living things, plants are formed mainly of water, and without it they soon die. Plants absorb water through small, hairlike roots. The moisture moves into larger roots, then to stems and eventually leaves. From there it passes through small pores called stomata, mainly found on the undersides of the leaves, into the atmosphere. This is known as transpiration, and as well as keeping the plant cool, firm and upright, it enables it to absorb food from the potting mix. More houseplants die through excessive or insufficient watering than for any other reason. Judging when to water is a skill derived from experience, but in recent years specialized equipment has taken the guesswork out of this task.

Above: To see if a clay pot needs watering, tap it with a cotton reel, or bobbin, attached to a short stick. The pot rings if water is needed, but makes a dull sound when it is wet.

Below: Moisture-indicator strips, also known as watering signals, are relatively new. Insert the strip into the potting mixture; the strip will indicate whether any water is required.

Above: Rubbing a finger or thumb on the potting mixture to assess its moisture content is the most popular method of judging if water is needed. However, repeated pressing tends to compress the potting mixture.

Below: The color of the potting mix is a good guide to watering. When dry, it becomes pale and crumbly, but if wet it is dark. Eventually, most houseplant enthusiasts use this method to assess if water is needed.

WATERING A PLANT

Plants vary in their need for water. Large ones need more water than small ones, while in winter and when dormant they need less water than in summer. Large plants in small pots need more frequent watering than small plants in large pots. There are two main ways to water houseplants.

Above: *Watering 'over the rim' means filling the space between the potting mixture and the rim of the pot. Allow the excess water to filter through to a saucer, emptying it after half-an-hour.*

Below: *Soft and hairy leaves are damaged if water falls on them, so stand the pot in a bowl of water until moisture reaches the pot surface. Remove the pot and allow it to drain.*

Above: *Moisture-meters are widely available and indicate when the potting mixture needs water. They are very efficient and precise, but repeated insertions of the probe eventually damage the plant's roots.*

Watering houseplants

When garden plants are watered, the excess moisture soon percolates downwards and unless the area is waterlogged, the roots do not drown or become deprived of air. However, potting mixture quickly dries out in summer, while in winter, when a plant is not growing rapidly, it may become waterlogged if over-watered. Both dry and water-saturated potting mixture cause plants to wilt. An inspection soon reveals the cause.

Leaves are the food-producing parts of plants. They use carbon-dioxide from the atmosphere, in combination with water absorbed by the roots, to create growth. This process is activated by sunlight and is known as photosynthesis. Water also passes into the atmosphere through the stomata (see page 22), mainly found on the undersides of leaves. Water given off in this way is known as transpiration.

Water, together with plant foods, pass into the large roots, then to the stems and later into the leaves. Some plants have long stems, while others have leaves that appear to develop from a point level with the surface of the potting mixture or soil.

Healthy roots are vital to a plant's survival. Large roots hold the plant firmly in the soil or potting mixture, while fine ones absorb water, as well as the nutrients mixed in it. The water then passes through the larger roots on its way to the stems and leaves.

see page 22

SAVING A DRY PLANT

1 Plants deprived of water wilt, eventually reaching a point when, no matter how much water is given, they never recover. Leaves and stems first become soft, then dry and crisp.

SAVING A SATURATED PLANT

1 If the potting mix is saturated, the plant's leaves become limp. Eventually, slime covers the potting mixture and diseases infest the plant. The lower leaves are the first to become diseased and unsightly.

2 *Plants can be revived if you take rapid action. If the plant has flowers, cut them off. Stand foliage* plants, such as this Ficus benjamina, *in a bowl of water until bubbles cease to rise from the dry potting mix.*

3 *Mist-spray the leaves several times to reduce the plant's need to absorb water to replenish moisture* lost through transpiration. Place the plant in light shade for a few days and allow it to recover.

2 *Knock the pot rim on a firm surface and remove the plant. If the rootball is packed with roots it will retain its shape, but if it is sparse there is a risk that it may fall apart. Take care not to damage the roots.*

3 *Use absorbent kitchen paper to soak up excess water from the rootball. Repeated wrappings may be necessary to remove the water. Check for the presence of root mealy bugs, which resemble small woodlice.*

4 *Leave the rootball wrapped in paper until dry (but not bone-dry) and crumbly. If the rootball is packed with roots, it is better to leave it unwrapped and exposed to the air to allow excess moisture to evaporate.*

5 *When the rootball is dry, pot up the plant into a clean pot with fresh potting mixture. Resume normal watering, but take care not to saturate the mixture continually, as the plant may be seriously damaged.*

Humidity

The amount of moisture in the air influences the health and growth of plants. Most plants need a humid atmosphere if their leaves and stems are not to become dry.

The perceived humidity of air is closely related to the temperature. The higher the temperature, the larger the amount of moisture it can hold. In winter, when the air is quite dry, rooms in which the temperature is high can, as far as plants are concerned, become like deserts. Mist spraying is an excellent way of increasing humidity around houseplants in summer, but make sure you spray at the right time of day, namely in the morning, so that moisture has a chance to dry before the onset of night. Never spray in the evenings, especially in the fall and winter. Avoid spraying when the sun is shining, as water globules act as lenses, intensifying the sun's rays and burning the leaves.

Humidity levels

If humidity is too high, soft leaves soon decay, especially if hairy. Leaves that clasp stems create traps for water. Flower petals, especially when tightly packed together, become covered with furry mold. Plants with masses of soft leaves closely packed together become infested with decay. If humidity is too low, the tips of leaves become shriveled, curled and brown. The whole plant wilts if the temperature is very high, with leaves eventually falling off. Flowers fade and discolor, buds wilt and eventually fall off. Tips of shoots wilt, then shrivel.

KEEPING THE ATMOSPHERE HUMID

Above: *Regularly mist-spray smooth-surfaced leaves in summer. Take care not to spray water onto the flowers, as they then soon decay. Place a piece of card in front of flowers.*

Above: *A few plants, such as philodendrons and the Swiss cheese plant, have aerial roots that must be mist-sprayed in summer to prevent them becoming dry and hard.*

Double potting

Some foliage houseplants can be given both a humid atmosphere and cool roots by potting them in two pots, one inside the other. A layer of moist peat between the pots protects the potting mixture from excessive warmth, while the moist peat creates humidity around the leaves. Only use clay pots for double-potting, as the cooling is created by the evaporation of moisture through the sides of pots. This does not happen in plastic pots.

Left: *Placing plants in groups creates humid microclimates around them, as the moisture given off from the leaf surfaces is trapped. Displayed alone, a plant soon loses its moisture.*

1 Select a clay pot about 2in(5cm) wider than the clay pot in which the plant is growing. Place moist peat in the base and put the smaller one inside. The two rims must be level.

2 Fill the space between the pots with moist peat. You may need to compress the peat with a small stick. Ensure that the inner pot is in the center of the outer one.

3 Moisten the peat between the pots. Allow excess water to drain, ensuring the peat is not totally saturated. Regularly check that the peat is moist, especially in summer.

Repotting a houseplant

When plants fill their pots with roots, you must repot them. If you neglect this task, the plants become stunted and will not achieve their full size. When the potting mix is filled with roots, excess moisture is rapidly absorbed and given off by the plant through its leaves. This prevents the potting mix being completely saturated and eventually makes it totally unsuitable for plant growth. Move plants progressively and in small stages from one pot to a larger one. If small plants are moved into pots that are too large, their roots are surrounded by masses of potting mixture and it is difficult to keep the moisture content at the right level.

Below: Many cacti have stiff and sharp spines and need careful handling. When repotting them, use gloves or hold the plant firmly by encircling it with folded newspaper.

1 *A few days before repotting a plant, water it thoroughly. If the rootball is dry it will take longer to* establish. Tap the rim of the pot on a firm surface, while supporting the rootball with the other hand.

3 *Place some potting mixture in the base of the pot, so that the surface of the rootball is about 0.5in* (1.25cm) below the rim of the new pot. Then trickle potting mixture over and around the plant's rootball.

2 *Check that the roots are healthy and not infested by root pests, such as root mealy bugs (see page 38). Select a clean pot that is slightly larger than the previous one.*

4 *Gently firm the potting mixture around the rootball until it is 0.5in(1.25cm) below the rim. Later in the plant's life, when repotting into a large pot, leave more space at the top.*

5 *Water the potting mix 'over the rim' (see page 23), rather than by standing the pot in a bowl of water.*

Watering overhead settles the potting mix around the roots. It is essential that they are in close contact. To

improve the plant's appearance, place the growing pot in an attractive outer container, known as a cache pot.

Feeding and topdressing

Plants need a balanced diet of nutrients if they are to remain healthy and live for a long time. Most plants underachieve, as they are usually starved. Regular feeding during the growing period can make a remarkable difference. Foliage and summer-flowering houseplants are normally fed at 10-14 day intervals from early spring to late summer while they are growing strongly. Feed winter-flowering plants at about 14-day intervals while they are in flower. Plants need different amounts of foods at certain stages in their development; phosphates for a strong root system, nitrogen for masses of leaves and stems and potash for a wealth of flowers.

Young houseplants will need feeding once they have used up the nutrients in the potting mixture into which they were initially planted. Liquid fertilizers are the traditional and most common way to feed houseplants. Follow the manufacturer's guidelines; never use more than recommended.

1 Dilute concentrated liquid fertilizer in clean water as directed. Do not experiment with the concentration – it may kill your plants.

2 Thoroughly agitate the water, ensuring that the fertilizer is completely mixed. Use it before the plant food has had time to settle.

3 Water the plant carefully. If the potting mixture is dry, first water it. If you apply fertilizer to dry potting mixture, there is a risk of the fertilizer damaging the plant roots. In addition, if the mixture is dry, the rootball contracts and leaves a gap around the inside of the container, through which water and fertilizer will escape and be wasted.

Right: *If a plant has smooth (not hairy) leaves, it will benefit from a light misting with a weak mixture of water and liquid fertilizer.*

Other feeds

Fertilizer pills and sticks *are pushed into the potting mixture and provide food over several months. They are best used in spring and up to midsummer. If applied late in summer and into fall, they provide food when some plants should be resting. Fertilizer pills and sticks concentrate the nutrients in one place and encourage an uneven spread of roots. However, they are easy and clean to use.*

Foliar feeds *are diluted with clean water and applied through a mist-sprayer. As well as absorbing nutrients through their roots, some plants are able to take in foods through their leaves. They usually respond quickly to foliar feeds and so the technique is best used as a quick, reviving tonic. Only apply foliar feeds to plants with smooth, non-hairy leaves. Avoid spraying the flowers. Take care not to mist-spray plants when they are standing in strong sunlight, otherwise the leaves*

Above: *Gently push a feeding stick into the mix, about 0.5in(1.25cm) from the side of the pot, where most of the feeding roots are situated.*

Below: *Pills can also be inserted into the potting mix. Some devices enable you to insert the pills without having to dirty your hands on the mix.*

TOPDRESSING LARGE HOUSEPLANTS

1 When plants in pots become too large to be repotted, topdress them in spring. Allow the surface potting mixture to dry out slightly, then use a small trowel to scrape away the top 1-2in(2.5-5cm).

2 Replace the surface scrapings with fresh potting mixture. Leave a space between the top of the mixture and the rim of the pot, so that you can water the plant when the potting mixture becomes dry.

FEEDING AIR PLANTS AND BROMELIADS

Above: *Air plants (tillandsias) are adapted to live in humid places. Feed them by misting the leaves with a weak solution (about a quarter of the normal strength solution) of a liquid fertilizer once a month from spring until late summer.*

Above: *Many bromeliads have urns at their centers, through which they are watered and fed. Once a month, from spring to late summer, pour a weak solution (about a quarter of the normal strength) of a liquid fertilizer carefully into the urn.*

THE BENEFITS OF FEEDING

Above: *Feeding houseplants regularly makes a remarkable difference. These two Mexican hat plants (Kalanchoe daigremontiana) were propagated at the same time. The one on the left has not been fed, other than with the nutrients present in the potting mixture when it was initially planted. The plant on the right has been fed regularly every 14 days.*

Grooming and care

Grooming plants is a vital part of growing houseplants. Removing dead blooms extends the flowering period, and pinching out shoot tips encourages a neat and attractive plant. Supporting and training stems also keeps plants looking tidy. At the same time, you will soon notice any signs of disease or pest damage and can take swift remedial action.

2 When the shoots of young plants are 10-18in(25-45cm) long, insert the support into the potting mixture. Pliable canes can be pushed into the mix, but attach plastic loops to the rim of the pot.

1 From early fall to late spring, pink jasmine (Jasminum polyanthum) creates a wealth of white or pale pink flowers, usually trained around a large hoop of pliable canes, or a white or green plastic loop.

3 Carefully curl and train the shoots around the support, taking care not to bend or kink them. Repeat this task several times throughout summer, and regularly feed the plant to encourage growth.

CLEANING LEAVES

Dust and dirt are the enemies of leaves, spoiling their appearance, clogging pores and preventing the sun reaching them. Proprietary, ozone-friendly sprays are ideal for cleaning large-leaved plants. Clean hairy-leaved types and bristly cacti with a small soft brush.

1 Support large leaves with one hand and gently wipe them with a damp cloth or spray them with a leaf cleaner. Do not do this in strong sunlight, as the leaf will scorch.

2 Clean plants with many small leaves by gently swirling them in clean water, allowing the excess to drain. Dry them in gentle warmth, away from direct and strong sunlight.

3 Remove dirt and dust from bristly cacti and hairy-leaved plants by using a small, soft brush. Blowing strongly on the leaves while brushing also helps to remove dirt.

LOOKING AFTER FLOWERS

Check flowering houseplants regularly when they are in bloom and remove any dead flowers. Decaying flowers left on plants encourage the others to rot, and the decay may then spread to the soft leaves. Removing dead flowers also encourages the development of new blooms.

1 Pinch off the dead flowers from azaleas. Do not leave any part of the flower, as this encourages the onset of decay around soft shoots. Hold the shoot firmly with one hand while pinching off with the other.

2 Pull off the stems of cyclamen flowers that have faded and started to wither. Hold the stem firmly and tug sharply, so that it comes away from the base of the plant. Do not just remove the flowers.

TRIMMING STEMS AND SHOOTS

Occasionally, the stems of some plants with a sprawling, scrambling or climbing habit need trimming. Always trim them back to a leaf joint, using a sharp knife, secateurs or scissors, or just hold the stem firmly and snap it sideways. Never leave behind a short piece of stem, as this only encourages the onset of decay.

1 Trim slightly woody stems, such as those on azaleas, with sharp scissors, cutting back to a leaf joint. This encourages bushiness and the development of sideshoots.

2 Encourage young plants to form a bushy base by nipping back young shoots to leaf joints. If this job is neglected, plants become bare at their bases and unappealing.

Maintaining houseplants while you are away from home

If your carefully nurtured houseplants die through neglect while you are away from home it is a major disaster. A plant's main requirement will be water, and a neighbor will often act as a 'plant-sitter', but inexperienced plant-sitters tend to overwater and it may be safer to rig up your own watering system. The result of overwatering is that roots rot and the plants die, sometimes weeks after you return home. The length of your absence, as well as whether it takes place in winter or summer, influences the treatment given to the plants. However, there are steps you can take to ensure the survival of your plants for several days or even a few weeks.

Before leaving home

A week before leaving home, check your plants for pests or diseases. If necessary, spray them immediately. Before long absences, spray all plants, as some pests may be at their egg stage. If left unsprayed, such plants will be smothered with adult insects by your return. Place large plants in saucers of water on a plastic sheet in the center of a room, away from sunny windows. Draw curtains, especially those on sunny windows, during summer. Keep small plants moist and cool for short periods by placing them in plastic seed trays and packing moist peat around them. Close the door of the room in which the plants are left, to prevent drafts drying them. Arrange for a friend to turn symmetrically shaped foliage plants a quarter of a turn every few days to prevent them becoming lopsided.

PREPARING PLANTS

1 *Remove all faded flowers, as well as those that will be past their best by the time you expect to return.* If left, they decay and encourage the rest of the plant to deteriorate, especially if it has soft leaves.

2 *Remove dead leaves from foliage plants. Those with masses of foliage are soon damaged by decaying leaves that are left in place, and the rot quickly spreads.*

3 *Place small plants on a capillary mat, one end spread over a draining board and the other trailing* into a sink full of water. The sink acts as a large reservoir. This irrigation system is ideal for long absences.

4 *Use wicks to water plants individually. Push one end of the wick into the potting mixture and the other end deeply into a reservoir of water that is taller than the plants.*

5 As well as placing plants in bowls of clean water, you can also stand them on moist pebbles of expanded clay particles in shallow dishes. Both of these methods also increase the humidity. Avoid placing the containers in drafts, as this encourages the plants to use up their reserves of water very rapidly.

Houseplant pests

Prevention is much easier than trying to eliminate an established colony of pests or a severe infection from a disease. It is far better to take a few preventative measures, such as buying plants from reliable and reputable sources, inspecting all new plants as soon as you get them home and isolating and treating them immediately if necessary. Do not plant houseplants in garden soil, which may be infested with pests and harbor disease spores. Instead, use properly prepared potting mixture. Check plants regularly, perhaps when watering them, to ensure that they are clean, and remove dead flowers and leaves, as they encourage disease. Active pests, such as aphids, whitefly, thrips and red spider mites, soon pass from one plant to another. Slow-moving pests often hide under leaves or in leaf joints, as well as under pots. Pests of potting mixtures are difficult to detect, their presence only becoming apparent after the damage has been done. Always check rootballs for pests when repotting plants and do not use infected plants as propagation material.

When using any chemical treatments, always follow the maker's instructions. Using chemicals at higher concentrations than those recommended seldom improves their effectiveness and may even damage some plants. Check that the chemical will not damage susceptible plants, such as succulents, palms and ferns. Do not mix two different chemicals, unless recommended, keep all chemicals away from children and pets and do not transfer chemicals into bottles that children might believe to hold a refreshing drink. Use only chemicals recommended for indoor houseplants. Remove all food and fruit from where sprays are used and do not spray wallpaper or fabrics. Do not assume that pest-killing insecticides developed from natural plant extracts are not dangerous. Wash out all containers, pipes and sprayers with soapy water after use and do not use the same equipment to spray insecticides and weedkillers. Do not spray plants in strong sunlight. Do not allow pets to lick or chew plants that have been newly sprayed; many chemicals have a residual effect lasting for several weeks. Do not spray plants if pets are in the room, but take the plant outside to treat it. Caged birds and fish in tanks are also very susceptible to chemical sprays.

Above: Gently push an insecticidal stick into the potting mixture, a little way in from the edge of the pot. Take care not to damage the roots.

Above: Lightly dust the leaves with the insecticide. Avoid creating large blobs of dust on one leaf, while leaving others devoid of insecticide.

Using insecticides

There are several ways of applying insecticides: spraying, dusting or pushing insecticidal sticks into the potting mixture. Insecticidal sticks are a preventative measure, while spraying and dusting are better if the plant is totally infested. Several sprays and dustings are usually needed in order to kill all the insects.

APHIDS
Aphids are also known as greenfly, blackfly, aphis and aphides.
Description: Small, soft-bodied, sap-sucking insects, usually green but may be gray, orange or black.
Damage: Aphids mostly attack the soft parts, such as petals, shoot tips and young leaves. They pierce the tissue, sucking sap and causing mottling and distortion. Aphids excrete a sticky substance known as honeydew, that is not only unsightly, but also encourages the fungal disease sooty mold (see page 40).

Above: *Place the plant in a large plastic bag before spraying it. Do not spray flowering plants, as the blooms may then be damaged.*

Houseplant pests

Control: Spray plants as soon as you see the pests, using insecticides containing dimethoate, malathion, pirimiphos-methyl with pyrethrins, or resmethrin and pyrethrum. Repeat spray every 10-14 days.

CYCLAMEN MITES

These pernicious pests attack a wide range of houseplants, including cyclamen, pelargoniums, African violets and busy Lizzies.

Description: Minute, eight-legged, spiderlike creatures that cluster on the undersides of leaves and look like a coating of dust. Young mites are almost transparent, adult females vary from milky white to brown.

Damage: Leaves curl from the outside and become wrinkled into depressions and pockets. Infested foliage becomes darker than normal and the flowering period is shortened. Flower buds often fail to form and those that do develop are distorted and fall off. Check corms kept from the previous year. Spray with malathion or insecticidal soap.

RED SPIDER MITES

Red spider mites attack carnations, chrysanthemums and other ornamental plants.

Description: About the size of a pinhead and varying in color from a transparent yellow-white through green to orange and brick-red. In winter the color tends to be red, whereas in summer when females are breeding they are lighter in color.

Damage: Both adult and immature mites pierce and suck the undersides of leaves, causing a fine, light mottling on upper surfaces, which becomes yellow and blotchy in severe attacks. Mites often create webs.

Control: Daily mist spraying of plants prevents an attack developing into epidemic proportions, but do not syringe flowers or soft and hairy leaves. Spray with derris or insecticidal soap as soon as you find evidence of the spiders or the damage they have caused. Remove and burn seriously infected plants.

MEALY BUGS

Mainly subtropical and tropical pests. Plants attacked include palms, ferns, vines, azaleas and hippeastrums.

Description: White, waxy, woodlice-like creatures that live in groups. If ignored they form large colonies.

Damage: Suck sap, causing distortion, loss of vigor and yellowing of the leaves. Like aphids, they excrete honeydew, encouraging sooty mold (see page 40). They form colonies in leaf joints, along stems and on leaves.

Control: Wipe off light infestations with a cottonbud dipped in methylated spirits. Spray established colonies with malathion. Burn seriously infested plants.

ROOT MEALY BUGS

These are closely related to mealy bugs, but instead of attacking leaves, stems and shoots, they infest roots. They mainly live on the outer roots of plants in pots, especially infesting cacti and other succulents.

Description: Resemble waxy woodlice.

Damage: Chew roots, especially small ones. Normal root functions are upset, resulting in the discoloration of foliage and wilting plants. If left untreated, plants will die.

Control: Inspect roots when repotting plants. If a plant wilts or becomes discolored for no apparent reason, remove the pot and check the roots. Drench the roots and rootball with a solution of malathion. Repeat several times, at 10-14 day intervals.

SCALE INSECTS

The range of scale insects is wide, and plants attacked include orchids, ferns and other ornamental houseplants indoors, as well as in greenhouses and sunrooms.

Description: The first sign of attack is when plants become sticky. There is evidence of swollen, protective, waxy brown discs under which the female scale insects produce their young.

Damage: Suck sap and produce honeydew that encourages the presence of sooty mold (page 40).

Severe infestations cause speckling and yellowing of the leaves.

Control: Young scale insects at the 'crawler' stage are the easiest to kill. Wipe them away with a cottonbud dipped in methylated spirits. Malathion also kills 'crawlers', but eradicating established colonies is difficult and plants are best burned.

WHITEFLY

These pests are a particular nuisance in greenhouses and sunrooms, infesting a wide range of plants. Tomatoes and cucumbers in greenhouses are often attacked.

Description: Mothlike, 0.12-0.25in (3-6mm)-long, insects with wings and a white, mealy covering. When disturbed, they flutter about the host plant. Mostly found on the undersides of leaves.

Damage: Young green nymphs suck sap and excrete honeydew, encouraging the presence of sooty mold. Leaves turn yellow and fall off, as well as becoming black and messy through sooty mold.

Control: Eradication is not easy, and several sprayings at 3-5 day intervals are necessary. Spray with malathion or pyrethrum.

THRIPS

Several types of thrips infest plants in sunrooms and greenhouses, although they are not major pests of indoor plants.

Description: Tiny, dark brown, flylike creatures, about 0.12in(3mm) long, with light-colored wings and legs. Often seen jumping or flying from plant to plant.

Damage: Thrips feed by piercing and sucking leaves and flowers, causing silvery mottling and streaking. In severe infestations, the flowers are distorted. The undersides of leaves develop small globules of a red liquid that eventually turns black, creating an unsightly mess.

Control: Spray with malathion or derris, repeating the treatment several times. Infested plants in dry potting mixture suffer the most.

Above: Aphids, or greenfly, are the most common pest of plants and can make them unsightly. If not eradicated, aphids soon spread to other plants.

VINE WEEVILS

Serious pests, both as larvae and in their beetlelike, adult form.

Description: Adult weevils are similar to beetles, but have a short snout. Each weevil is 0.3-0.5in(8-1.25cm) long, black, and covered with short hairs that create a matt, dull appearance. Larvae are fat, legless and creamy-white, the head is brown, with mouthparts adapted for chewing roots. Invariably, the larvae are seen in a semi-curled manner.

Damage: Roots, tubers, bulbs and rhizomes are seriously damaged by the larvae, causing wilting and, eventually, death. Adult weevils chew flowers, stems and leaves.

Control: Immediately you see the larvae or adults, water the potting mix with malathion or a soil pest killer and spray the leaves.

EARWIGS

These pests attack outdoor plants, as well as those in greenhouses and sunrooms.

Description: Familiar pests.

Damage: Feed at night, chewing and tearing leaves and flowers.

Control: Spray with malathion, although it is often easier to pick them off. Shaking flowers and leaves in the morning soon dislodges them.

SLUGS AND SNAILS

Not usually pests of houseplants, but plants stood outdoors on patios in summer may harbor them when taken back indoors. Plants in sunrooms and greenhouses may also become infested.

Description: Familiar pests.

Damage: They crawl and leave trails of slime, chew flowers, stems, shoots and leaves, as well as roots, tubers, bulbs and corms. They feed mainly at night, hiding under pots, boxes and plant debris during the day.

Control: Pick off and destroy. Alternatively, in greenhouses place small heaps of slug and snail bait around affected plants. Hide these under tins or slates to prevent cats and dogs eating them.

Houseplant diseases

SOOTY MOLD
Black sootylike mold that lives on the honeydew excreted by aphids and other sap-sucking insects.
Damage: Leaves, stems and flowers become covered with honeydew, then sooty mold. At first, the black, sooty deposit appears in clusters, but soon spreads and merges until the whole surface is covered.
Control: Spray aphids and other sap-sucking insects. Wipe away light infestations with a damp cloth.

RUSTS
Complicated diseases, seldom infesting plants indoors, but frequently seen on carnations and chrysanthemums in sunrooms and greenhouses.
Damage: Raised rings of brown or black spores. Rust permeates the tissue, reducing a plant's vigor.

Control: Remove and burn any infected leaves. High humidity in sunrooms and greenhouses encourages rusts, so increase ventilation. Do not propagate from infected plants.

VIRUSES
Viruses are microscopic particles that invade plants and animals, causing disorder in the tissue but seldom killing their host.
Damage: Only the results can be seen, varying from deformed growth and mottled and streaked leaves to color changes in flowers.
Control: There is no treatment for virus-infected plants. Remove and burn damaged growth. Spray against sap-sucking insects, such as aphids. Buy only plants that are clean and healthy, and do not propagate from infected plants.

Above: *Pelargonium with leaf curl virus.*

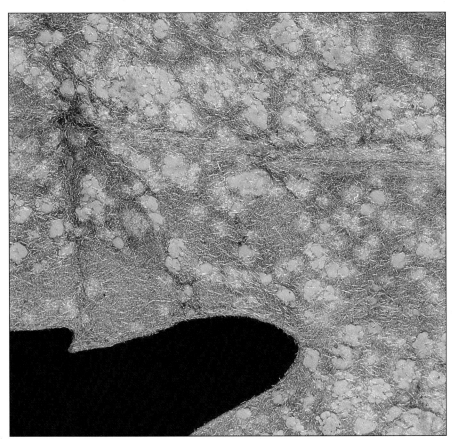

Below: *Rust on a chrysanthemum leaf.*

Above: *Botrytis on a cyclamen.*

BOTRYTIS

A fungal disease, also known as gray mold. Spores in the air enter plants via wounds or decaying tissue.
Damage: Gray, furry mold on soft young leaves, shoots and flowers.
Control: Cut off and destroy infected parts. Remove dead flowers. Damp, still air and overwatering encourage gray mold. Spray with a fungicide.

BLACK LEG

A disease mainly of cuttings, especially pelargoniums.
Damage: Stem bases become soft and black.
Control: Cold, wet, compacted and airless potting mixes create conditions suitable for infection. Infected plants and unsterilized potting soil are also a source of infection. Remove and destroy seriously infected cuttings. Slightly infected tissue can be cut away from valuable cuttings. Reinsert cuttings in clean potting soil. Make sure that there is good air circulation over the cuttings and keep the potting mixture barely moist.

DAMPING OFF

Attacks seedlings soon after germination. May also attack established plants in greenhouses and sunrooms.
Damage: Seedlings, especially those that have been sown too thickly, turn black and collapse.
Control: Sow seedlings thinly in well-drained potting mixture. Place them in a well-ventilated position and make sure that the potting mixture is not excessively wet. At the first sign of damping off, remove infected seedlings, lower the temperature and improve the air circulation.

POWDERY MILDEW

A fungal disease that produces a white, powdery coating over leaves, often on both sides.
Damage: White spores are unsightly and soon disfigure plants. Appears in spring and summer. Infects leaves, flowers and stems.
Control: Remove badly infected leaves, stems and flowers. Increase ventilation; keep the atmosphere drier.

Above: Black leg on a young pelargonium.

Below: Botrytis (gray mold).

Above: Powdery mildew on a begonia.

41

Physiological disorders

As well as being harmed by pests and diseases, plants also become damaged and unhealthy because they are not grown properly.

WILTING

Growing houseplants in pots throughout the year and maintaining the right degree of moisture in the potting mixture is not easy. A houseplant's need for water varies throughout the year. The size of the plant, the size of the pot and the amount of potting mixture it holds all influence the frequency and amount of water needed for healthy growth.

Too little water is the main cause of wilting. Without rapid remedial action (pages 24-25), the leaves and flowers reach a point where, no matter how much they are watered, they do not recover, and leaves become crisp and brittle.

Too much water is just as likely to cause wilting, especially in winter when plants are less active and need less water. Excess water encourages the onset of decay; leaves become soft rather than brittle. If plants are not badly affected, withhold water until the potting mix dries out and follow the advice described on pages 24-25.

There are other causes of wilting. For example, during very warm summer days – usually in late afternoons – houseplants with large amounts of foliage and growing in small pots may wilt slightly, even though the potting mixture is moist. This is because the plant is unable to absorb sufficient moisture to replace that lost by evaporation through the leaves. If the plant recovers by late evening or early morning, do not worry about the wilting.

Some soil pests, such as root mealy bugs, graze on roots and make plants wilt. Remove the pot and check the rootball. If pests are present, drench the potting mix thoroughly with a proprietary insecticide.

LOSS OF FLOWER BUDS

This may happen if plants are in a draft or a dry atmosphere, receive a sudden chill or are knocked. Throw away any flower buds that fall, because if left, they encourage the development of diseases.

LOSS OF LEAVES

Occasionally, leaves fall off. If this happens quickly, it could be that the plant received a shock, such as a sudden drop in temperature or being placed in a cold draft. Reposition the plant in an even, moderate temperature away from drafts.

If leaves become yellow and slowly fall off, it is because the plant was given too much water and the potting mixture became waterlogged. Keeping plants in dark positions – especially when this is combined with a lack of plant food such as nitrogen – also causes leaves to become yellow.

Remove fallen leaves and do not give the plant further water until the rootball has become moderately dry.

GREEN SHOOTS ON VARIEGATED PLANTS

If green shoots appear on variegated plants, it is usually because the plant is in too dark a position. Move the plant into a brighter spot.

Occasionally, green shoots appear on a variegated plant, even when it is in good light. This is known as reversion and you must cut out the offending shoots at their bases.

DAMAGED LEAF SURFACES

If leaves become crisp and brown, it is due to insufficient water. But if white or straw-colored patches or spots appear, it is usually because water was splashed onto the leaves while the plant was in strong sunlight. The moisture then acted as a lens and intensified the sunlight. However, damage can also occur if plants that do best in slight shade are placed in direct sunlight, even if there is no water on their leaves.

Plants that can be left in full sun in a sunny window in winter will soon become damaged if left in the same position in summer. Soft-leaved plants are soon damaged in this way.

Above: Some plants that have been deprived of water develop crisp, brown areas on their leaves, especially along the edges.

Above: Plants with flowers or berries are soon damaged if deprived of water. Leaves become dry and crisp and hang in an unsightly manner.

Above: *A lack of light soon causes leaves to become yellow, especially the lower ones that are furthest from the source of light.*

Above: *The soft leaves of the African violet are soon damaged if water droplets fall on them and the plant is left standing in strong sunlight.*

Above: *Some of the leaves on this bougainvillea have fallen off due to a sudden drop in temperature. Keep the plant at a constant moderate temperature.*

Part Two

HERB GARDENING

The most convenient place to grow herbs is where you use them – in the kitchen. Nowadays stores sell pots of all the most popular herbs, such as chives, basil and chervil, specially so that you can keep them in the kitchen window, ready to use. But for a bigger range, visit a garden center or a specialist herb farm. Here you will find more unusual kinds, such as lemon basil, French tarragon, orange thyme and pungent Greek oregano, all of which add an extra zest to your cooking. If you use a lot of fresh herbs, it is a good idea to grow your own plants from seed. Instead of using pots, a good, productive, but space-saving method is to grow herbs in in small plastic trays filled with seed mixture. This way there is no need to sow, prick out and pot up individual plants. Simply sow the seed thinly and start snipping the young plants as soon as they are big enough.

The plants keep producing new shoots, so each tray can be cut several times before it needs replacing with a newly sown one. Many herbs used for cooking have other household uses, which make them doubly valuable. Pots of mint and lemon grass grown in the kitchen deter flies. Eau-de-cologne mint has a delicious smell that is released every time the leaves are gently squeezed. As well as using it in cooking (with peas or new potatoes), it makes a very pleasant natural air freshener. This section explores some of the practical techniques involved in raising, propagating, planting and preserving some popular indoor herbs.

Left: Herbs make decorative and useful subjects for containers indoors.   *Right: Sage can be used fresh or dried.*

Propagating herbs by sowing seed indoors

Growing herb plants from seed has several advantages: annual varieties can be replaced every year, there are considerable cost savings and you will have access to a far wider variety of herb species and varieties. Most specialist herb seed stockists will mail supplies to their customers. The disadvantages are that, as with any plants grown from seed, you cannot guarantee that the new plants will be identical to the parent. Also, you may be left with many surplus plants, although you can usually sell or exchange these. Annual varieties with a long growing season are best started off indoors. Using this method, you can control the growing conditions, such as soil, temperature and light. You may even consider buying a purpose-made propagator to keep seeds ideally protected, ventilated and heated. To avoid the risk of 'damping off' – a condition in which young seedlings die off – use a sterilized potting mixture. White mold on the surface of the soil is a warning sign of this fungal infection. Watering with a weak infusion of chamomile can sometimes halt the condition before it progresses too far.

1 Small individual pots may be made of biodegradable fiber or reusable plastic. Fill them with a sterilized potting mix and water well.

2 Sprinkle a few seeds into each pot, using your fingertips for fine seeds. If the seeds are larger, press a couple of them lightly into the surface of the mix.

3 Arrange the pots in a propagating tray and top with a fine layer of vermiculite or sterilized potting mix, sprinkling it with your fingers to avoid making the layer too thick. Water lightly.

Carefully label all pots and trays for future reference.

4 Plant up larger trays in the same way, providing they have suitable drainage holes. Fill with about 1.6in (4cm) of sterilized seed potting mix, moisten well and sprinkle with seed.

5 Finish off with a fine layer of vermiculite or seed mix. Use an empty pot for better control over larger areas. Moisten with tepid water.

6 Cover the tray with paper, glass or a ventilated plastic cover. Leave it in a warm place or turn on the heat if the propagator is an electrically operated model.

7 Check the trays and pots every day or two and make sure the mix remains moist. Move them to a light situation as soon as the first seedlings appear.

When the seedlings are large enough to handle, prick them out carefully into a deeper seed tray or peat pots.

Taking soft semi-ripe cuttings

1 This bushy branch of red sage will provide plenty of material for cuttings. Examine it for signs of disease or pests and remove any thrips or whitefly by washing under running water. Select healthy, undamaged young branches.

Many plants, including sage, marjoram, pineapple sage and lavender – in fact almost any herb that you wish to increase – will root well from cuttings taken at any time from late spring to early summer. Select healthy shoots at the right stage of growth, i.e. when the current season's shoots start to harden at the base. Test the shoot between your fingers. If it breaks, the shoot is either too soft or too hard. If it springs back when you let go, the shoot is at the right stage. On sage plants, as with many other herbs, the central growth on each branch is usually more advanced than the side shoots. Selecting this stem for propagation will encourage a bushy, attractive plant. If you are propagating from one of the colored sages (golden, purple or variegated), make certain that you select the shoot with the best coloration on the plant. In this way, you can be sure of maintaining good, well-colored plant stock. Remove any excess leaves on the stems, leaving about two leaves below the central leaf tips. If the cutting has too many leaves, it has to work to keep them firm with moisture. This can delay or prevent the more important task of forming roots for the new plant.

2 Start by removing the lower leaves to expose the stem. Usually a gentle tug is all that is needed, but you can use a sharp knife for the task if necessary.

3 Remove all the leaves on the stem except for the tip leaf buds and the two leaves beneath. This will expose the soft new season's growth.

4 Cut through the stem at the point where the 'wood' is beginning to harden, just above the small stalks of the previous year's growth.

5 Make a hole with a dibble and insert the cuttings. These cuttings are being placed into pots, but a deep seed tray is just as suitable. Rooting in pots allows the cuttings plenty of room for root growth. Cuttings in trays will need to be potted on at an earlier stage, once rooting is established.

Use a potting mixture with an open, gritty texture.

This dibble is custom-made, but the blunt end of a pen or pencil will serve equally well.

Taking tip cuttings from small plants

Small, shrubby plants, such as thyme, grow soft tips and stems from the woody, mature growth made during the previous season. These tips will root easily if taken between early summer and the onset of fall. Select a suitable bunch of soft growth from the plant and place it immediately in a plastic bag out of direct sunshine to prevent any loss of moisture from the leaves. Label each bag if you are taking cuttings from different plants, as it can be difficult to identify them later. The potting mixture for cuttings must be gritty to provide plenty of spaces for air and water to percolate, and free-draining, to encourage rapid root growth. Rooting will take place in four to six weeks in a covered, heated propagator. It will be slower, but just as successful, if you support a plastic bag with three or more sticks or wire hoops over the tray. When new growth appears, ventilate the bag with a few holes, gradually increasing the number of holes over several days, before removing the bag completely.

2 Thoroughly water the tray about two hours before planting to allow excess water to drain away. Insert the cuttings 2in(5cm) apart in a tray or put 4-6 cuttings in a 4in(10cm) pot.

Cut off young shoots with a sharp knife.

1 Trim pieces to 2-3in(5-7.5cm) by cutting through the semi-soft stem above a woody section. Remove the lower leaves.

3 *Always label the finished tray with the plant name and date, especially if you have taken plenty of cuttings. A final mist spray will refresh the leaves and also helps to 'settle' the soil.*

Cuttings from different plants can share the same tray, as long as their aftercare is similar.

Rooted cuttings

After four weeks, the simple cuttings of thyme shown at the far lefthand side of the photograph have started to develop. The potting mix has been shaken off the cuttings on the righthand side to show the first fine roots. Most roots develop at the base, but a few may grow from the sides. When lifting rooted cuttings from the seed tray or pots, try to retain as much undisturbed mix as possible, as this encourages quick, healthy growth when the cuttings are potted on.

4 *Cover the propagator with the lid, leaving the vents open. Put it in a warm place, but out of the sun.*

Planting up a parsley pot

Parsley is probably one of the most used herbs in the kitchen; a vital ingredient in stuffings, marinades and bouquet garnis, and invaluable as a garnish. However, it does not dry well, becoming virtually tasteless, so it is well worth growing it yourself to ensure a fresh supply. Parsley can be chopped and frozen for adding to soups, stews and marinades, but you can still eat it fresh throughout the winter by sowing seeds under glass in midsummer or by potting up the roots of spring-grown plants to bring indoors. Bear in mind that cropping plants by the handful rather than the sprig can quickly outstrip supply. The attractive terracotta pot shown here has room for four plants, which will provide a bigger crop. A partly shady spot is ideal for parsley and be sure to provide plenty of moisture. Parsley is a biennial and the leaves taste best in the first year, becoming bitter and rather coarse in the second, so try to sow a fresh supply each year in spring and late summer. The seeds can take at least six weeks to germinate, but this can be speeded up by soaking them overnight in warm water and then soaking a fine tilth seed bed with boiling water before planting. Cover the seeds thinly with fine seed mix and thin the seedlings to about 10in(25cm) apart.

3 *Once you have released each plant by upturning and tapping the pot, you may need to squeeze the rootball slightly to make it fit through the holes in the parsley pot. Avoid damaging the roots.*

Support the plant gently in your hand as you make it ready for planting.

The dense foliage of curled parsley (Petroselinum crispum) looks best in this kind of container.

1 *Place a few crocks or broken pieces of china in the bottom of the pot to ensure that the drainage holes do not become blocked.*

2 *Fill the pot with potting mix until you nearly reach the level of the planting spaces – in taller pots, these might appear at various heights.*

4 Insert the parsley plants into the planting holes, pressing them firmly into the potting mixture. Make sure that the rootball is covered and the plants are the right way up.

Parsley seeds or seedlings are both suitable for planting.

5 Place the final plant in the top of the container, making sure that it is planted at the correct height to grow right out of the top.

6 After filling and firming with potting mixture, sprinkle a handful of small stones or gravel on the surface to reduce moisture loss.

7 The finished pot provides plenty of parsley for picking within a very small planted area. Pinch off flower stalks as they appear to maintain good growth.

The versatility of mint

The mint family contains many varieties of great cooking and medicinal value. When grown in the open garden they spread vigorously, but in pots they make compact fragrant plants for a window indoors, porch shelf, or sunroom. The best varieties of mint to use as potplants are those with variegated foliage such as pineapple mint and ginger mint, or with the best scent such as eau-de-cologne mint (all three can also be used for cooking). Curled spearmint, basil mint and lemon mint are useful decorative and useful varieties well worth growing on the kitchen window. Look out too for novelty mints such as chocolate mint, occasionally available from specialist herb farms, which are best used as scented-leaved plants. By keeping them warm in winter, mints continue growing all year round, instead of dying down as they do in the garden. Either move new potgrown plants into bigger pots during the spring or summer to bring indoors, or dig up dormant roots in fall or early winter. Within a few weeks of potting, watering and moving indoors, these spring back to life. If sprigs are snipped regularly for kitchen use, potted mint stays neat and tidy; otherwise cut long stems back close to the top of the pot when necessary to keep the plants compact.

The curled spearmint has unusual, deeply veined leaves.

Spearmint (Mentha spicata) is the most common mint.

The Corsican mint (Mentha requienii) makes a dense carpet of miniature leaves and flowers.

Black spearmint has bold purple stems and purple-tinged leaves.

Lemon mint has a fresh lemon scent, which is useful for cooking and also in cosmetics.

The buddleia mint has an upright habit and attractive soft, green foliage.

Spicy ginger mint (M. x gentilis 'Variegata') has pretty green foliage.

The pennyroyal (Mentha pulegium) prefers a damp, shady spot.

Creeping forms of pennyroyal make a wonderful scented carpet of small leaves.

Red raripila (M. raripila rubra) has a spearmint flavor.

Peppermint (M. x piperita) has a refreshing mint flavor and antiseptic properties.

Bowles' apple mint has unusual thick, gray, feltlike leaves and a fresh apple scent.

Above: *An ingenious way of growing a whole collection of mints is to plant them in a variety of terracotta pots of different sizes, thus displaying their range of color, shape and texture.*

55

Chives – with a hint of onion

You can grow chives from seed or you can buy them from herb stockists. However, being a member of the onion family, perennial chives are usually propagated by dividing the bulbs and you should do this every three years in any case to regenerate the plants. Simply remove the plants carefully from the pot and gently separate the bulbs before planting them out in new containers. The potting mix must be rich and damp, but chives are not too fussy about sun or shade. Sometimes the spiky, green, hollow leaves begin to look a little yellow and this means the mix has become too impoverished or possibly too dry. Using good-quality potting mix or being more conscientious about watering is the answer, especially when the chives are grown in a container. Their spiky shape can make an effective contrast against other, leafier herbs and yet they only grow about 12in(30cm) tall, which makes them a good choice where space is limited. Snip the leaves with a knife or scissors throughout the summer to provide an interesting green garnish and a mild onion flavor to virtually any savory dish. The flowers appear in early summer – fluffy mauve pompons on the top of strong, hollow stalks. It is a good idea to nip these off despite their attractive appearance, to encourage good leaf growth.

Giant chives (Allium schoenoprasum sibiricum)

Chives (Allium schoenoprasum) *the smallest of the onion family.*

Right: *Children might enjoy growing chives in a novelty pot or container, usually made of terracotta, where the spikes and flowers make a focal point.*

Allium perutile, *the everlasting onion.*

56

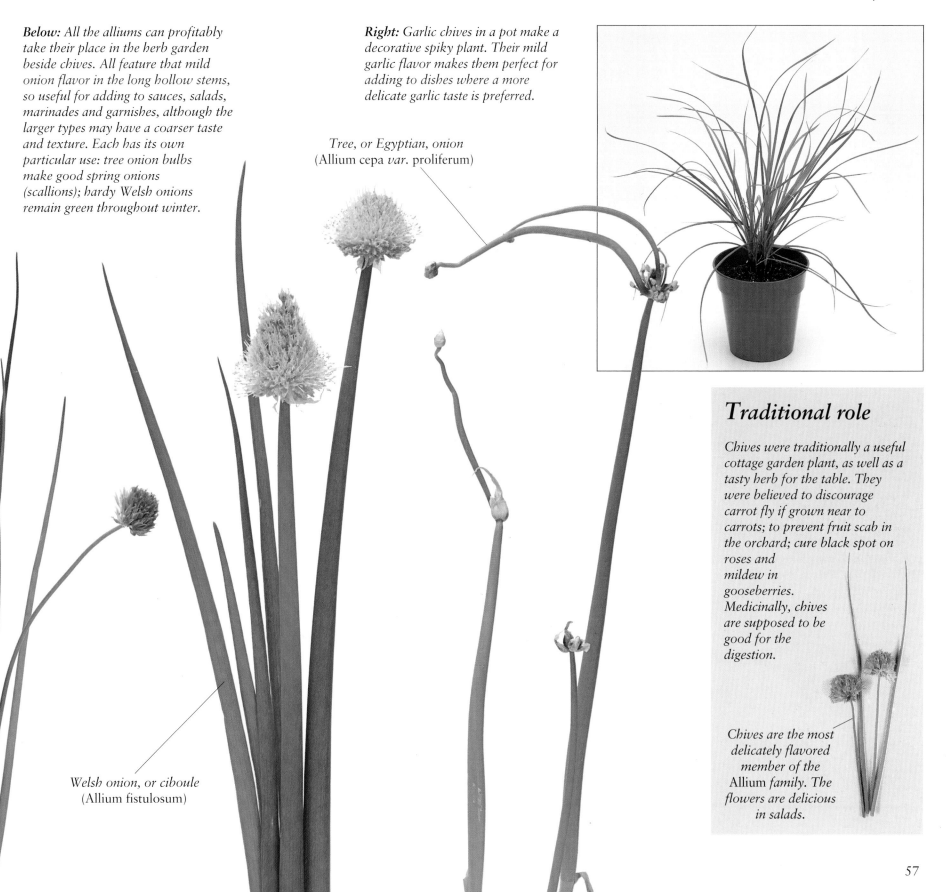

Below: *All the alliums can profitably take their place in the herb garden beside chives. All feature that mild onion flavor in the long hollow stems, so useful for adding to sauces, salads, marinades and garnishes, although the larger types may have a coarser taste and texture. Each has its own particular use: tree onion bulbs make good spring onions (scallions); hardy Welsh onions remain green throughout winter.*

Right: *Garlic chives in a pot make a decorative spiky plant. Their mild garlic flavor makes them perfect for adding to dishes where a more delicate garlic taste is preferred.*

Tree, or Egyptian, onion
(Allium cepa *var.* proliferum)

Welsh onion, or ciboule
(Allium fistulosum)

Traditional role

Chives were traditionally a useful cottage garden plant, as well as a tasty herb for the table. They were believed to discourage carrot fly if grown near to carrots; to prevent fruit scab in the orchard; cure black spot on roses and mildew in gooseberries. Medicinally, chives are supposed to be good for the digestion.

Chives are the most delicately flavored member of the Allium *family.* The flowers are delicious in salads.

Basil – a Mediterranean taste

An aromatic native of India, basil is well worth growing as an annual in cooler climates for its wonderful flavor; dried, it has a completely different taste. Basil is too tender for the general herb garden, but it may do well during the summer on a sunny, well sheltered patio with other tub-grown herbs. You could grow it under glass in a sunny, protected corner or in the greenhouse with plenty of rich potting mix among the sweet peppers, eggplants and tomatoes. Regular watering and pinching out the top shoots are essential for good bushy growth. Basil is usually grown from seed in early spring to give as long a growing season as possible. Sow the seeds indoors or in a heated greenhouse and keep the potting mixture well watered. Once they are big enough, transplant the seedlings into individual pots or boxes for growing indoors or in the greenhouse. The potting mix should be well drained but moist, rich yet not heavy. Harvest continually during the growing season by cutting back the top and side shoots to the second pair of leaves. Left to its own devices, basil produces long spikes of white or purplish flowers from midsummer onwards.

1 *Pinching out the top growth of basil is essential if you wish to create a well-shaped, bushy plant. This is best done with the fingertips.*

Piquant pesto

Basil is perfect with tomatoes and most hearty savory dishes. Try chopping and steeping the leaves in oil or vinegar as a flavoring. Make pesto sauce by pounding fresh basil leaves to a pulp and mixing them with garlic, olive oil, parmesan cheese and ground pine kernels or walnuts. Use in pastas, soups or herb and garlic bread.

Below: Basil is available in a surprising variety of types and colors, from tiny-leaved Greek basil to purple forms with large crinkly leaves.

Bush basil (Ocimum minimum)

Sweet basil (Ocimum basilicum)

Red/purple ruffles basil (Ocimum basilicum 'Red Ruffles')

Greek basil (Ocimum minimum *Greek variety*)

Bush basil (Ocimum minimum)

Dark opal basil (Ocimum basilicum purpurea)

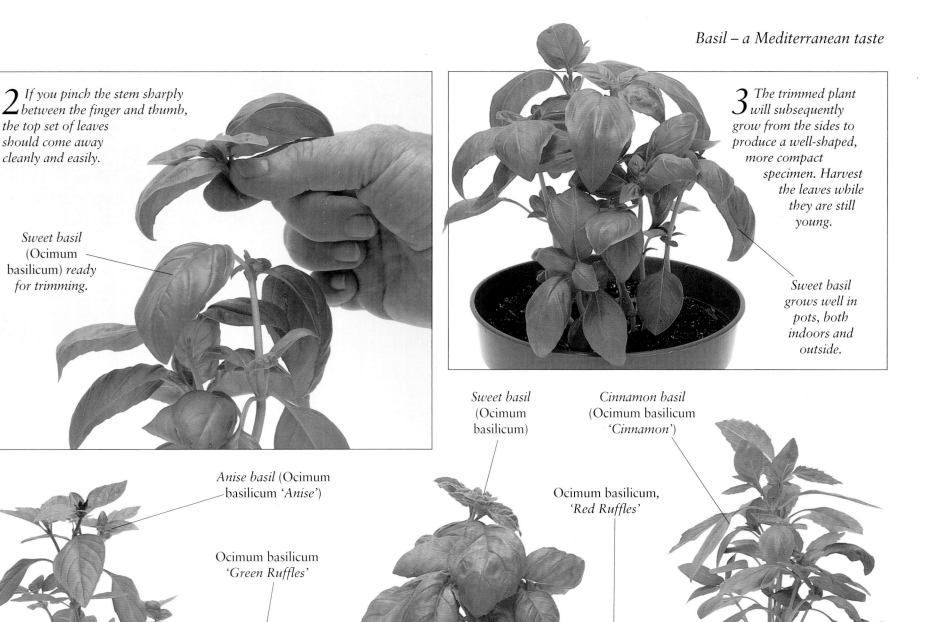

2 *If you pinch the stem sharply between the finger and thumb, the top set of leaves should come away cleanly and easily.*

Sweet basil (Ocimum basilicum) ready for trimming.

3 *The trimmed plant will subsequently grow from the sides to produce a well-shaped, more compact specimen. Harvest the leaves while they are still young.*

Sweet basil grows well in pots, both indoors and outside.

Sweet basil (Ocimum basilicum)

Cinnamon basil (Ocimum basilicum 'Cinnamon')

Anise basil (Ocimum basilicum 'Anise')

Ocimum basilicum, 'Red Ruffles'

Ocimum basilicum 'Green Ruffles'

Creating a herb garden for the window

A windowbox is the perfect way to grow a selection of culinary herbs in the minimum of space. The kitchen window is an obvious site, providing the window opens conveniently enough for regular access to your mini garden. Make absolutely sure that the windowbox is firmly secured; use strong brackets or ties and check these periodically for wear or weathering. The box might be homemade from new or old timber, painted to match window frames or shutters; or it might be lightweight plastic, antique stone or terracotta. If the windows are too exposed a site, why not plant up an indoor windowbox, perfect for a few of the more tender species, such as basil. Regular cropping or trimming is important to ensure that the herbs remain small and leafy. Keep the box adequately watered and apply a liquid feed during the growing and cropping season. The soil soon runs out of essential nutrients in the confines of a box, especially where plants grow prolifically and where rain washes constantly through the soil. A mulch of small pebbles conserves moisture and reduces the effect of heavy rains.

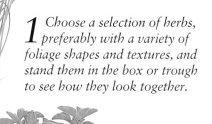

1 Choose a selection of herbs, preferably with a variety of foliage shapes and textures, and stand them in the box or trough to see how they look together.

2 Take out the plants again and arrange a few crocks or broken pieces of pot in the bottom to prevent the potting mixture washing away.

3 Add 2-6in(5-15cm) of washed gravel or pea shingle to make a well-draining layer at the bottom of the box. Top up with planting mix.

4 Plant the herbs, keeping to your original plan and maintaining a balance of appearance, height and habit. Tip them gently out of their pots and into your hand, supporting the stem lightly between your fingers.

5 Top up with soil, making sure it settles between the plants without any air gaps. Do not fill right to the top of the box to allow for watering.

6 A sprinkling of gravel or small stones on top of the soil around the plants looks attractive and helps to slow down moisture loss.

Herbs in the kitchen

The flavor of fresh herbs is far more delicate than that of dried ones, so use them generously. Generally speaking, add them at the end of cooking for maximum effect. Mint, basil and tarragon change their flavor once dried, so do not expect them to taste the same as before. Add fresh, chopped herbs with a swirl of cream to homemade soups; sprinkle them on salads; tie them in tiny bundles to add to stocks and stews; or tuck sprigs of rosemary, sage or thyme under the roast joint with a slice of unpeeled onion and a clove of garlic to bring out the flavor.

Chives
(Allium
schoenoprasum)

Thyme
(Thymus vulgaris)

Sorrel (Rumex acetosa)

Sage (Salvia
officinalis)

French tarragon
(Artemisia dracunculus)

Parsley
(Petroselinum
crispum)

Oregano
(Origanum vulgare)

7 The finished trough looks good and includes a useful blend of flavors for the cook. If you use plenty of herbs in cooking, reduce the number of plants in the box to two or three bigger plants.

61

Freezing herbs

We are so familiar with the idea of drying herbs to preserve them that we often forget that most of them can be stored very successfully in the freezer. In fact, for some herbs, such as parsley, basil and tarragon, freezing is by far the best option, as their flavor changes quite dramatically when they are dried. Frozen herbs can be chopped and added to soups, stews, marinades, sauces – in fact to any dish – but they cannot be used as a garnish. Pick the herbs fresh and sort them out to remove any dead or withered parts. Then arrange them in sprigs. You need not blanch them, but give them a quick rinse in cold water and dry them on kitchen paper or a clean tea towel to remove any small insects. Freeze them in small quantities, making sure the bags are well labeled. For convenience, you may like to put together some useful combinations, such as a bouquet garni mix or, say, parsley, chives and tarragon for adding to egg or fish dishes. To use the herbs, chop them in their frozen state as soon as you remove them from the freezer. Instead of freezing herbal mixtures in sprigs, you could chop them finely together and freeze them in ice cubes to pop into stews and sauces. Herb flowers, such as borage, can be frozen in the same way for adding to drinks.

2 Combine the chopped herbs and sprinkle a little of the mixture into each compartment of the ice cube tray. You may need extra trays if you are freezing large quantities.

Marjoram

Thyme

Parsley

Sage

1 Herb mixtures frozen in ice cube trays are so convenient for adding to stews, soups and sauces at any time of year. First chop the herbs finely with a sharp knife or herb mill.

Herb flowers in ice

Some herb flowers, such as borage and salad burnet, are traditionally added to summer drinks. Freeze the flowers in filtered or bottled water; chemically treated tapwater tends to go cloudy when frozen.

3 *Top up the container, ideally with filtered or bottled water, and place the tray in the freezer. The herb cubes will remain usable for several months.*

Freezing individual fresh herbs

Freeze individual herbs in small sprigs. When you are ready to use them, shred them off the stem while they are still frozen.

1 *Gather the herbs and lightly wash the trimmed sprigs in clean water to remove any dirt or small insects.*

2 *Absorb any excess moisture by patting the sprigs gently with a piece of kitchen paper or a clean tea towel.*

3 *Package the herbs ready for freezing in individual plastic bags. Squeeze out as much air as possible, fasten and label clearly.*

Drying herbs

Although it is possible to grow a few of the more compact herb varieties in pots on the window to carry you through the winter, this will rarely keep pace with demand if you are a keen herb user. Drying your own herbs enables you to continue using them all year. However, some herbs are simply not worth drying; evergreens, such as thyme, for example, should be fine for cropping right through the winter, while parsley, chervil and fennel simply do not dry well, losing all their flavor in the process. Drying herbs is quite simple. When you have harvested and sorted them, just tie them in bunches and hang them in any shady but warm and well-ventilated place, such as an attic or shed. The quicker the herbs are dried, the better the color and flavor and the less chance there will be of them going musty. Some people use a well-ventilated airing cupboard successfully or dry herbs in a cool oven with the door ajar. Another traditional method is to use a drying cupboard, where the herbs are set out on meshed trays. This is a useful strategy for flowerheads. It is also possible to buy an electrical version for quicker and more predictable results. Once the herbs are dried, strip the leaves from the stems and store them in airtight containers. To dry seeds, collect the seedheads just before they ripen and dry them in bunches upside down with a cloth or paper below to catch any seeds that fall. Strip the rest of the seedheads from the stalk and leave them to dry out completely for another week or so before storing.

Lemon balm

Santolina

Rosemary

1 Gather your chosen herbs for drying and lay the sprigs or branches all facing the same way. Tie the stalks together loosely into small bunches with string, twine or cotton.

2 *Hang the bunches to dry in a warm, airy place away from direct sunlight. A barn or attic is ideal. The bunches should hang freely or they will take too long to dry and become dusty.*

Santolina

Rosemary

Lemon balm

3 *When the herbs are dry, shred them off the stalks, taking care not to crumble them too much or they will not retain so much flavor. Some leaves, such as bay, can be stored whole.*

4 *Store the dried herbs in glass or ceramic jars with tight-fitting lids. Label them clearly and keep them away from direct light. Replace dried herbs every twelve months.*

Dried herbs around the home

Dried herbs are useful when fresh ones are not available, particularly those that do dry successfully, such as rosemary, sage, thyme, mint and lemon balm. Some, such as fennel, dill, cumin and coriander, are better when the seeds are dried and stored. Remember that dried herbs have a more intense flavor than fresh ones, so you will only need a pinch or a teaspoonful, rather than a bunch of leaves. Dried herbs also make refreshing herbal teas and household products, such as mothbags and small scented bags. Scented dried herbs include lavender, clove carnation, roses, santolina, scented pelargoniums, bergamot and woodruff.

Part Three

GARDENING IN THE SUNROOM

A sunroom is a unique combination of garden and living room. It opens up endless new possibilities for using plants decoratively, allowing climbers and houseplants to achieve their full potential since they have space to grow naturally. And it provides facilities for cultivating plants that you may never have been able to grow before, such as exotic orchids, tender fruits or even tropical water lilies in an 'indoor' pond. You can make the sunroom whatever you want. Tip the balance in favor of gardening by growing plants on tables, shelves and up the walls and even over the roof. Washable floors, plenty of opening ventilators and some means of shading are vital ingredients for a 'green' sunroom mix. Unless the sunroom is heated by radiators from the domestic heating system, add a greenhouse heater for winter use. If you favor a 'glass living room', choose fewer plants – perhaps two or three large striking specimens or some smaller houseplants that will enjoy sunroom conditions, growing in pretty pot covers. Leave the central area free for indoor entertaining; choose furniture that will withstand heat and exposure to bright sun. Add roof fans and decorative blinds to keep the atmosphere comfortable on sunny days. However you use the sunroom, you will have fun rearranging plants, and inventing new combinations of plants, 'props' and furnishings to create stunning new interior landscapes, time after time.

Left: Fuchsia denticulata *is an easy subject to grow.* **Right:** Hedera canariensis *'Montgomery' will thrive in a sunroom.*

67

Climbing plants for the sunroom

A sunroom is essential if you wish to grow tropical or subtropical climbers in temperate climates. Without this protection, non-hardy species, such as *Bougainvillea, Beaumontia, Stephanotis* and some of the thunbergias, as well as unusual climbers, such as the spectacular gloriosa vines, will die in temperate climates during the winter. It is not unusual for people to grow passion flowers or grape vines in a sunroom, but it is not entirely necessary in temperate climes, as they may grow so enthusiastically under glass that they cause a space problem. The best way to grow a grape vine in the sunroom is to plant it outside and to unleash all its growth entirely inside. Black-eyed Susan vines, or *Thunbergia alata*, make excellent sunroom plants with their creamy, white, yellow or orange colors and rounded leaves, but do not confuse them with black-eyed Susan, or *Rudbeckia alata*, which is an herbaceous perennial. There are at least 100 species of *Thunbergia* to choose from; another favorite is *T. grandiflora* which, like all the thunbergias, is a native of South Africa and Madagascar. It has blue flowers, hence its common names of sky vine, blue sky vine and blue trumpet vine. All these thunbergias are best grown as annuals and encouraged to climb up arbors, trellises, and over porches.

Right: *Madagascar jasmine (Stephanotis floribunda) has very elliptical leaves and fragrant, white, waxy flowers that last a long time. It will twine up trellis in a sunroom and also makes a good houseplant.*

Above: Gloriosa rothschildiana *has superb red petals with wavy yellow edges. The plant can cover a well-lighted wall, with flowers appearing regularly from the foliage.*

Left: *The bleeding heart vine, (Clerodendrum thomsoniae) is a twining evergreen shrub from tropical Africa. Its interesting white and crimson flowers are ideally displayed on a trellis - inside in temperate climes.*

Right: *The Australian, late winter-flowering bower plant (Pandorea jasminoides) has white flowers with pink throats, but there are all-white and pink cultivars, as shown here.*

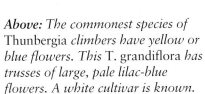

Above: *The commonest species of* Thunbergia *climbers have yellow or blue flowers. This* T. grandiflora *has trusses of large, pale lilac-blue flowers. A white cultivar is known.*

Right: *Setting the mood (and scent) in this sunroom is a jasmine arch over a trompe l'oeil depicting a classic urn and pedestal, with the stylish addition of green garden furniture.*

Growing clematis in the sunroom

The rise in popularity of sunrooms has resulted in the availability of a range of suitable plants. Clematis are eminently suited to growing in a sunroom and this allows you to experiment with some of the less hardy varieties. Some of the more common varieties usually grown outside also make good sunroom plants. The early large-flowered hybrids, such as 'Barbara Jackman', will flower a month or so earlier than normal, while the spectacular blooms of *Clematis florida* 'Sieboldii' can continue well into the winter. The winter-flowering *Clematis cirrhosa* and its varieties do well outside, but never flower so successfully in colder latitudes. In a sunroom they provide an abundance of pale yellow flowers, some with deep red markings, that provide color during the cheerless winter months. Bear in mind that pests and diseases can flourish in sunrooms, so inspect your plants regularly and apply any relevant treatments.

Above: *When grown in the protected environment of a sunroom, varieties such as 'Bees Jubilee' will flower much earlier than usual, but provide them with some shade or their blooms will fade to a dingy white.*

Left: *Clematis x* cartmanii *'Joe' is a relative newcomer from New Zealand. It is not completely hardy outdoors in temperate climates but grown within a sunroom, it will produce a mass of white flowers.*

Suitable clematis

Clematis x cartmanii 'Joe'
Clematis cirrhosa
C. c. balearica
C. c. 'Freckles'
Clematis florida 'Sieboldii'
C. f. 'Alba Plena'
Clematis forsteri
'Comtesse de Bouchaud'
'H.F. Young', 'Lasurstern'

Left: *Sunrooms are superb places to grow plants, but it is vital to keep them scrupulously clean, as a variety of pests and diseases are likely to flourish in the warm, humid conditions that prevail there.*

Below: *Clematis 'Lasurstern' produces pure blue flowers for most of the summer. If the plant is grown in a container, you can move it outside for the winter and replace it with another variety that will flower at this time.*

Foliage plants

Foliage plants provide a good all-year-round sunroom display; use them on their own or make them the backdrop to an ever-changing tapestry of flowering plants. Since foliage plants tolerate shadier conditions than flowering kinds, they are ideal for a sunroom that has to be built on the sunless side of the house; choose ferns for the shadiest places. Large-leaved plants, such as palms, monstera and philodendrons, are the perfect way to create a rich tropical-looking landscape. Grow a few large, impressive specimens with pots of smaller, colored-leaved plants, such as maranta, calathea, solenostemon and begonia, to fill in fine detail. All these plants associate well with tropical flowering plants such as anthurium and orchids. This type of display needs light shade, constant heat and high humidity to succeed; it is no good turning the heat down in winter, as tropical plants such as these need a minimum of 60-66°F(16-19°C) to stay happy.

In a cooler sunroom, use near-hardy plants, such as aspidistra, ivies, *Oxalis triangularis*, fatsia and fatshedera, with the various asparagus ferns to create the leafy look; use chlorophytum or rhoicissus in hanging containers and make tabletop displays of small plants, such as tolmiea and *Saxifraga stolonifera* (mother-of-thousands), grouped together for added impact. Or use a mixture of gold, green and variegated soleirolia in a pretty container. The soft tree fern, *Dicksonia antarctica*, makes a stunning specimen plant for a sunroom that is only heated enough to keep out frost in winter.

Above: Phoenix canariensis *(Canary Island date palm) is one of the faster growing palms, best suited to a sunroom. It needs bright light to succeed.*

Hedera helix 'Pittsburgh'

Hedera helix 'Goldchild'

Hedera helix 'Annette'

Hedera helix 'Eva'

Above: *Ivies can be trailing, climbing, variegated or plain green. Train them round mirrors, over topiary frames or from baskets.*

Right: *The large leaves of* Fatsia japonica *make a striking background to flowering plants. This hardy evergreen plant is ideal for an unheated sunroom.*

Right: *A well-planted sunroom makes a pleasant place to sit and eat, or entertain friends. Metal furniture and a washable floor are practical and attractive options.*

Below: Aspidistra *tolerates a good deal of neglect but cannot survive overwatering. Clean the large leaves regularly to keep them looking good.*

Below: Cyperus *looks its best when grown standing in water, where you can see the reflections. It is one of very few plants that enjoys being grown this way.*

Above: *For the best display of yuccas, grow several of different heights together in the same container.*

Right: Begonia rex *have spotted and banded leaves, containing vivid metallic tints, but the flowers are insignificant.*

Foliage plants

In a hot, bright sunroom, you could start a collection of bromeliads, whose fascinating leaf patterns, shapes and colors create a wonderful display. Epiphytic types look best wired to pieces of cork bark or driftwood branches and hung up on a wall, while earthstars (*Cryptanthus* species) are best grown and displayed in a bottle garden or terrarium. Cacti and succulents, with their strange, often grotesque shapes, also make good collectables for a sunroom; stage them on shelves in matching terracotta or ethnic-decorated pots. On a table top, group plants needing similar growing conditions in large containers to make mini-landscapes, using knotty driftwood or pebbles and chunks of quartz rock for contrast. Create striking cacti and succulent displays in containers by embedding broken pieces of clay pots into the potting mix and adding a layer of decorative gravel.

Right: Succulents are trouble-tree plants for a sunny window; all except those with powdery coatings to the leaves can be stood outdoors in summer. In winter, keep them cool with little water.

Crassula ovata

Haworthia attenuata

Echeveria 'Perle von Nurnberg'

Echeveria 'Black Prince'

x Pachyveria hybrid

Right: Bromeliads such as this Guzmania 'Rana' are very resilient. Top up the central 'vase' with water all year round; keep the soil moist in summer but drier in winter.

Right: Cryptanthus, or earth stars, are another form of bromeliad; the leaves turn bright pink in bright sunlight. They are ideal for a terrarium as they like high humidity.

Sansevieria trifasciata 'Laurentii'

Right: *Asparagus fern* (Asparagus meyeri) *is ideal for a shady spot. If plants are well watered, the attractive foliage grows vigorously in summer and occasional sprays can be cut off to use for flower arranging.*

Above: *Spanish moss* (Tillandsia usneoides) *has no roots at all. It is a good subject for a humid sunroom, grown with tropical plants.*

Left: Sansevieria *is a very robust, slow-growing plant that needs good light, but not strong direct sun, and hates being overwatered. When happy, it produces strange green flowers.*

Below left: Calathea makoyana *has striking leaf patterns. It needs a warm, draft-free position out of direct sun, with constant high humidity.*

Below: *The rabbit's foot plant,* Maranta leuconeura *var.* kerchoveana, *needs high humidity, constant warmth and diffuse light.*

Sansevieria trifasciata 'Golden Futura'

Sansevieria trifasciata 'Golden Hahnii'

Flowering plants in the sunroom

The sunroom may need to play the role of a living room, a patio or a greenhouse. It provides the perfect opportunity to grow a huge range of tender and often exotic flowering plants, but usually has to accommodate other needs, too. When choosing plants, take into account the way the sunroom will be used. If it doubles as a dining room, living room or playroom, then houseplants such as hibiscus, gardenia and gerbera make ideal choices, since they are small enough not to get in the way of other activities, and since the room is in constant use, it is likely to be kept sufficiently warm for them in winter. If the sunroom is primarily used as a plant room, take advantage of the space to grow large dramatic plants, such as datura, strelitzia (bird of paradise), tibouchina and oleander. Climbing plants, such as plumbago, allamanda, jasmine, stephanotis and bougainvillea, can be trained on the walls, and exotic trailers, such as hoya or aeschynanthus, allowed to cascade down attractively from shelves or hanging pots hooked onto brackets in the roof. You could choose to grow exotic fruit, such as oranges, lemons, kumquat and figs, with passionfruit, grapes and kiwi fruit trained up over the walls and roof. As a general rule, true sunroom plants do not need such high winter temperatures, with 45-50°F(7-10°C) normally being adequate.

Above: A sunroom with a mixture of indoor plants, including a variegated weeping fig, and seasonal plants such as primulas and streptocarpus. An orchid and anthurium add a touch of style.

The bell-shaped flowers of abutilons come in a range of bright colors. If given enough light, plants bloom almost all year.

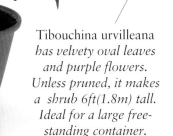

Lantana 'Radiation', a particularly striking color cultivar. Lantanas are prone to whitefly; the best non-chemical 'cure' is to stand plants outdoors for a few weeks in summer.

Tibouchina urvilleana has velvety oval leaves and purple flowers. Unless pruned, it makes a shrub 6ft(1.8m) tall. Ideal for a large free-standing container.

Bougainvillea is ideal for a hot, dry, sunny sunroom. It tolerates occasional neglect and in time, makes a big plant ideal for training up a wall. Plants need a cool dry winter rest below 50°F(10°C) to flower the following summer.

Pelargoniums also tolerate hot, dry, sunny conditions and occasional lapses in watering. Give them the same winter treatment as bougainvillea, and deadhead regularly in summer.

The summer flowers of oleander add a subtropical touch to a bright sunroom. Care for it in the same way as bougainvillea.

Aeschynanthus make good subjects for hanging baskets in a sunroom. Keep them humid in summer and shade from direct sun; in winter keep at 55°F(13°C). Cut back after flowering.

Allamanda cathartica is an evergreen climbing plant up to 10ft(3m) tall. Grow it in a large tub and train it up inside the roof or over a trellis.

Below: *Gardenia needs a warm room or the buds fail to develop. Keep plants humid, shaded from strong midday sun, and constantly moist. Pot in ericaceous mix. Use naturally soft water, or filter or boil and cool it to remove chalk.*

Flowering plants

The secret of success with sunrooms is to team plants to the environment, rather than trying to coax them to grow in unsuitable conditions. In a hot, bright sunroom grow sunlovers; many tender or fragile patio flowers, such as argyranthemum, diascia, *Anisodontea capensis,* and large-flowered, double grandiflora petunias, are ideal and will perform much better under cover than outdoors, especially if the summer is a poor one. In humid shade, choose impatiens, streptocarpus and episcia for color. The plants need not be grown in separate pots; in the same way as outdoors on a patio, those needing similar conditions can be grown decoratively in large planters to make them into more of a display. Alternatively, bank up plants on tiered staging or shelves on the back wall to make the most of their potential. Add seasonal flowers, such as primroses, cyclamen, indoor azalea, cineraria and calceolaria, to add temporary color in winter when few regular sunroom plants are in flower.

Left: Streptocarpus saxorum *is a compact trailing species that looks its best grown in a hanging basket in a sunroom. Cultivate as other streptocarpus; shade from direct sun and keep humid, with moist potting mix.*

Below: *Cacti tolerate occasional neglect, but when well cared for, many kinds like those shown here will flower regularly even while small.*

Cleistocactus strausii

Parodia scopa

Echinopsis chamaecereus

Mammillaria baumii

Above: *If it is happy,* Stephanotis floribunda *produces an abundance of superbly fragrant white flowers in neat clusters along the stems.*

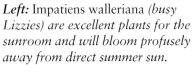

Left: Impatiens walleriana *(busy Lizzies)* are excellent plants for the sunroom and will bloom profusely away from direct summer sun.

Right: Clivia miniata *needs a cool winter rest below 50°F(10°C), with just enough water to prevent the evergreen leaves from drooping, to produce its brilliant flowers in spring. Plants flower best when potbound, so do not repot until absolutely necessary.*

Below: *The mauve-blue florets encircle the dense flower clusters of this* Hydrangea macrophylla *'Teller's Blue'. Hydrangeas will thrive in a cool, bright spot in the sunroom.*

Right: *When grown as a houseplant, the common white jasmine* (Jasminum officinale) *needs regular pruning to keep it under control. If its excessive vigor becomes a problem, you can plant it outdoors.*

Above: *Streptocarpus will flourish in a humid shady corner of the sunroom, bearing these elegant, trumpet-shaped flowers from spring through to fall.*

Right: Liquid feeds, including soluble feeds that are first diluted, allow you to feed more often when plants are growing faster. This tomato feed is useful for all fruiting and flowering plants.

Left: To prolong flowering, deadhead pelargoniums regularly. As soon as a flower is finished, snap the stalk cleanly away from the main stem of the plant as if 'picking' a flower. This keeps the plant looking tidy and prevents dead petals rotting and becoming a source of disease.

Scented-leaf pelargoniums

Scented-leaf pelargoniums are also suitable for the sunroom but look much less spectacular, as their flowers are mostly insignificant. They are grown for their aromatic leaves, which release their delicious perfumes into the air when gently crushed; according to variety, they may be scented of pine, spices, lemon, orange, rose or balsam.

Growing geraniums

There are several different types of geranium (correctly called pelargonium). The most popular for growing in a sunroom include zonal pelargoniums, which have kidney-shaped leaves, often with a dark band running round the middle; regal pelargoniums, which have large showy flowers and leaves with jagged edges; and miniature pelargoniums, which are small-scale versions of both these types.

All pelargoniums need dry air and plenty of direct sunlight to grow well. They are ideal for a sunroom that gets sun all day long and which can often be too hot and inhospitable for the normal range of sunroom shrubs. As soon as they start growing in spring, repot pelargoniums into fresh soil-based potting mixture. Avoid overwatering them, but feed them regularly with high-potash liquid tomato feed. Clean pelargonium plants regularly, removing brown or yellow leaves and dead flowers to keep plants tidy. Cuttings taken at any time from late spring to midsummer root easily in about six weeks. Pot them individually into soil-based potting mix. (Peat-based mixes hold too much water, which can cause plants to rot at the base.) At the same time, nip out the growing tip of each cutting to encourage plants to branch, otherwise they tend to grow straight up and become leggy. Alternatively, train a straight-stemmed cutting up a cane to form a standard plant, or train it as a fan to grow on the back wall of a sunroom.

Right: Pelargonium graveolens is one of the scented leaf pelargoniums, grown for its finely divided foliage that releases a strong citrus perfume when touched. This is its main attraction; the white or pale pink flowers are fairly small. It is easily grown from cuttings.

Below: 'Sancho Panza' is a miniature regal pelargonium with a naturally neat, compact, bushy habit and distinctive bicolor flowers. It blooms prolifically all summer and, given sufficient light, well into the fall.

Above: The large regal pelargonium has fine foliage and is taller and bushier than the small but floriferous 'mini-zonal'. Both are ideal for the sunroom.

Below: Red is the traditional color of zonal pelargoniums, but today they are available in a wide range of shades from white through pink to purple.

Propagating geraniums (pelargoniums)

1 Remove the lower leaves with a sharp knife. Make sure the blade is not in line with your thumb, so that you cannot cut yourself.

2 Make a clean cut across the base of the stem just below a node, or leaf joint. This is where the new roots will emerge.

3 Dip the base of each cutting in rooting powder. It contains plant hormones to assist with the formation of a strong root system.

4 Push single cuttings into a 2in (5cm) pot of seed mix, or put a few cuttings 1.5in(3.75cm) apart around the edge of a 4in(10cm) pot.

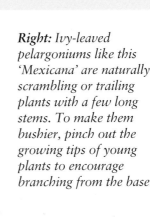

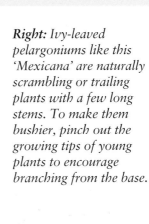

Right: Ivy-leaved pelargoniums like this 'Mexicana' are naturally scrambling or trailing plants with a few long stems. To make them bushier, pinch out the growing tips of young plants to encourage branching from the base.

1 *Cut a fully expanded but fairly young leaf with 1in(2.5cm) of stalk. In older plants, take a leaf towards the center of the plant.*

2 *Trim the base of the stalk with a very sharp knife, leaving a clean cut. Do not tear the skin or leave a jagged edge, which may rot.*

3 *Hold the cutting gently by one corner and dip the stem base into hormone rooting powder. This also contains a fungicide to prevent rotting.*

4 *Make a small hole and push the base of the stalk into a pot of seed mix, so that the leaf is just above the top of the mix. Firm the mix in gently.*

5 *Water in the cutting and stand the pot inside a loosely tied plastic bag supported with small canes. This will keep humid air round the leaves.*

6 *After 12-16 weeks, tiny plantlets appear at the leaf base. Remove the bag but wait until the plantlets are bigger before separating them.*

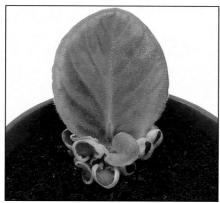

African violets

African violets are popular with collectors due to their huge range of flower colors and shapes. Miniature plants and some with frilly or bicolored flowers or variegated foliage are also available. New varieties are always being added to the list; find all the latest additions at specialist nurseries and flower shows. With care, African violets can be kept in flower for twelve months of the year. Plants need constant conditions: a steady temperature of about 65-80°F(18-27°C), good indirect light, and continuously high humidity. The easiest way to achieve this is to grow plants in a shaded sunroom and to stand them on a dish of damp pebbles, so that moist air rises up through the plant's leaves. Avoid drafts, sudden changes of temperature and wet potting mixture. African violets do not like to dry out entirely, but they grow much better in potting mix that is kept barely moist, rather than one that is too wet. The best way to water the plants is to stand the pots in tepid water for a few minutes and then let the surplus drain away before returning them to their trays. Avoid watering from the top, as this can encourage the neck of the plant to rot.

African violets do not have large root systems, so they do not need large pots. (In the wild they grow on rocks, often on their sides in crevices with very little rooting material.) Pots measuring 3.5in(9cm) will suit most plants and 5in(13cm) half pots are quite adequate for large, mature specimens.

Right: *Varieties with bicolored flowers, such as this candy-striped chimera-type 'Tineke', are new in African violet breeding. Expect to see many more colors in a range of flower types, including doubles and those with frilly flowers, appearing in the future.*

Above: *The white edging on these frilled purple flowers creates a picotee-style appearance on this attractive cultivar of African violet.*

Winter flowering

To keep African violets blooming in winter, make sure they receive adequate light; plants commonly start flowering again when they are moved closer to the glass. Alternatively, grow them under artificial lights, giving them 10 hours light in every 24 and keeping them close to the element so that the light level is sufficiently high.

Above: *Because they are small, it is easy to accommodate a varied collection of African violets.*

Below: *This chimera-type has single magenta flowers with a white frill round the edge of the petals. Like all African violets, it prefers to be slightly potbound; a 3.5in(9cm) pot will suit a plant of this size.*

Left: *No wonder African violets are so collectable. They are neat, compact and a symmetrical shape, and available in a range of types, colors and flower shapes.*

83

Left: 'Red Spider' makes a basket festooned with flowers for many months. Do not be deterred by the fuchsia's name, which may remind you of red spider mite; it produces an excellent display in a hanging basket.

Growing fuchsias

Fuchsias are reliable, frost-tender perennials, with showy flowers. In a sunroom, these are produced continuously from early summer until late fall. New plants can be bought at any time during the growing season, and are often available inexpensively as rooted cuttings. Though they can all be grown outdoors in summer, fuchsias make ideal plants for a sunroom as their large flowers are protected from weather damage, which often spoils them outdoors. The plants like good light, but need shading from strong direct sun; under glass this can cause the leaves to scorch.

Fuchsias are easily propagated from cuttings taken any time during the growing season; they root in four to six weeks. Choose non-flowering shoots or remove all flowers and buds from the chosen shoots first. Use a sharp knife to cut off the growing tip just above a leaf joint so that each cutting has two pairs of leaves. You can root them in a wide range of mediums, including blocks of flower foam as shown here. Keep fuchsias well watered, and feed them regularly with high-potash liquid tomato feed during the spring and summer. In fall, gradually reduce the amount of water. When plants shed their leaves keep them on the dry side and at a temperature of 40-45°F (5-7°C) for the winter. This 'rest' is essential for the following season's flowering, so do not attempt to keep plants growing all year round.

Fuchsia cuttings

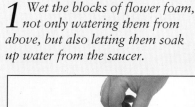

1 Wet the blocks of flower foam, not only watering them from above, but also letting them soak up water from the saucer.

2 Use a fine stick to make a small shallow hole in the foam blocks to hold the cuttings in position. Use the cuttings soon after taking them.

3 Hold each cutting by the leaves and insert one into each of the foam blocks. Do not force them in, as this could damage the stem.

4 The new roots will develop in about 10-14 days. Cuttings rooted in this way can be placed directly into a suitable potting mix.

Right: This variety of fuchsia, 'Lye's Unique', was bred in 1886 by James Lye. The waxy white of the tube and sepals was his trademark. It is still popular today and ideal for a sunroom.

Below: This is a species fuchsia, with the typical long tubes. The reason for this is not hard to understand, as the flowers are often pollinated by humming-birds with long tongues.

Above: It is easy to train fuchsias around a frame or hoop of plastic-covered wire, as here. This fuchsia is 'Whiteknights Pearl', a strong-growing cultivar, ideal for this purpose.

Pest control

Insect pests, particularly whitefly, are often a nuisance under glass. The easiest way to tackle these is to burn insecticidal smoke cones; the smoke percolates through the foliage much more effectively than spraying. However, make sure that the sunroom can be well sealed off from the house to prevent fumes coming into living rooms nearby. Alternatively, move plants out into the garden to spray them individually with a suitable pesticide, or use biological control by introducing a parasitic wasp (Encarsia formosa) into the sunroom in late spring. Before introducing new plants to the sunroom, put them in 'quarantine' for a few weeks and spray any pests that you discover to prevent infesting the whole collection.

Here, the parasitic wasps, Encarsia, have laid their eggs within the whitefly scales and turned them black.

A mature whitefly resembles a tiny moth, less than 0.04in(1mm) long.

These scales contain the immature whitefly.

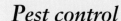

Above: Gentle spraying helps to create a humid atmosphere and you can also apply foliar feeds in this way; the plants take up the nutrients directly through their leaves.

Above: A lack of water results in soft limp leaves and wilted growing tips. Water the plant gently and empty the saucer after 30 minutes, rather than leaving the plant standing in water.

Above: You can use slow-release feeds in the form of pellets. Put these in the potting mix near the rootball. A large container, such as a hanging basket, may need two or three pellets.

Part Four

ENJOYING BONSAI

The two syllables of the Japanese word 'bonsai' literally translate as 'a tree in a pot', but when combined they acquire an altogether grander meaning. A bonsai is a plant that is established in an aesthetically harmonious container, and has been subjected to a number of horticultural and sculptural techniques in order to create a treelike image. At one end of the spectrum, these images are virtually exact replicas of their full-sized cousins. At the other end, they can become almost abstract sculptures, inspired by the landscapes of the mind.

A bonsai is not a naturally dwarfed variety, neither is it treated with any special potion to stop it growing larger. Its growth is not restricted by confining the roots in a pot, but by constant clipping and trimming. The size and shape are entirely determined by its keeper, whose horticultural and artistic skills also determine its eventual health and aesthetic quality.

A good bonsai does not have to be old. However, bonsai do improve with age. Bark texture, trunk taper, branch structure, fine twigs and so on do require time to develop, even with a helping hand. So over the years, with the right care and attention, a good bonsai can become a better bonsai. However, a poorly designed young tree can only become a poorly designed old tree, so it is essential to get the basic form right from the start. In this part of the book, you will find advice on buying healthy, well-shaped bonsai, an examination of the techniques involved in pruning and shaping bonsai, and guidance on watering and feeding the plants.

Left: *A stunning azalea with bicolored flowers.*

Right: *A dwarf pine growing in a rock crevice.*

Buying bonsai

Many newcomers to bonsai begin by being tempted to buy one at a garden center. The so-called bonsai offered for sale at garden centers are invariably tropical species from the Far or Middle-East. They may have been in stock for some time and be suffering from neglect. Tropical species cannot tolerate our climate, so they must be kept inside for most of the year. This is fine if you can provide a controlled environment, which is not easy. If you are intent on growing bonsai indoors, go to a reputable specialist nursery, whose plants will be well cared for and whose staff will be able to offer good advice. The same advice applies to buying hardy species. Specialist growers know their stuff, so benefit from their experience by asking as many questions as you can. Bonsai people are always glad to help. Meanwhile, the following points will help you get the best value.

Bonsai are expensive because it takes time to create them by hand, and they are transported half way round the world. Less than a reasonable price will only buy a 'half finished' bonsai, requiring several years' work to refine. It is best to buy any plant during the growing season so that you can be sure it is alive and healthy. If you buy in winter scratch the bark a little; if it is green underneath, the plant is alive; if not, it is dead. Avoid plants with die back, damaged leaves, etc., which may be symptoms of disease. Check that the tree is firm in its pot by holding the trunk and gently rocking it from side to side. If it moves put it back on the shelf. The trunk itself should have a natural shape and taper, with no unsightly scars of graft unions, and the surface roots should look natural as they emerge from the trunk. The soil in the pot should be loose and porous, moist but not waterlogged and should contain no established weeds. Liverwort and pearlwort are both signs of poor soil. The pot must have adequate drainage holes, which are not blocked.

Avoid bonsai with exaggerated spirals and hairpin bends; the branches should be evenly distributed around the trunk, the lower ones being thicker than those at the top. Make sure that there are no wire marks on the trunk or branches or, worse still, that there is no wire embedded in the bark. Always ask the nurserymen about the tree's horticultural requirements such as watering, feeding and so on, and try to find out when it was last repotted so you know when next to tackle this task.

What to avoid

The pine above is a three-year-old seedling that was pruned once at the end of its second year. The grower wired the trunk to make it look authentic, without altering the shape. Its only potential for bonsai is as raw material, needing to be grown in the ground for many years. The plastic pot reveals the nursery's desire for a fast buck. The little Japanese maple on the right is four years old. Its trunk has been shaped with wire by somebody who has clearly never seen a real tree! There is no way this freak could be turned into a bonsai. The only hope would be to cut the trunk below the first bend and start again.

Left: *Japanese cedar (Cryptomeria japonica).* **This magnificent bonsai is very ancient indeed, well over a hundred years old. Its trunk is hollow all the way up and the branches are by now very brittle.**

Above: *When you see trees presented like this you can be fairly confident you are getting good value. They are all healthy and weed-free, and the fertilizer pellets on each pot show they are well cared for.*

Repotting and root pruning

The thought of root pruning fills most bonsai novices with horror, but it is essential in order to maintain the tree's health and vigor. If the process is ignored your bonsai will become potbound. It will weaken, shed shoots and branches and eventually die. In the wild, a tree will extend its roots each growing season in much the same way as it produces new shoots. These new roots do most of the work, absorbing water and nutrients. As the tree matures, some older roots will die back, only to be replaced by strong, new ones. However, things are different in a pot. You have to reproduce this cycle artificially in order to keep your bonsai healthy. Health means vigor, and a vigorous tree is more able to resist disease and can outgrow attacks by pests. It will also respond better to training techniques. A healthy young bonsai – say up to ten years old – in a small pot will pack its container with roots within one season, so it will need to be root pruned each year. Older trees, especially conifers, tend to grow more slowly, taking perhaps up to five years to fill the pot. However, before you start to panic, remember that it takes time for problems associated with root confinement to take effect, and you can miss a year every so often without putting your tree at risk.

Just as the roots begin to grow in spring is the ideal time for root pruning. Although it is possible to repot at any time during the dormant season, the longer the wounds wait before they can regenerate, the more they are at risk of further damage from frost and fungal

1 After two years, the roots of this medium-sized trident maple are filling the pot, and need to be pruned. They are all healthy and have already started to grow. The fine, white vertical roots are from weed seeds that germinated over the winter.

2 Lift the tree from its pot and carefully comb out the roots. Work from the center outwards. Use a chopstick, knitting needle, or whatever else comes to hand.

3 Comb out the underneath of the root mass as well, without tearing it. When you have finished you should have removed about a third of the total volume of soil.

4 Trim back the roots so that the remaining root mass does not quite fill the pot. Use a pair of sharp scissors, but not your best ones, because of the grit in the soil!

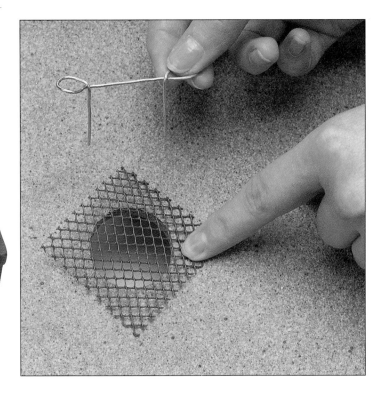

2 Push the wire through the mesh and drainage holes and bend the 'legs' up tight against the underneath of the pot.

5 Cover the grit with a layer of fresh potting mix. This must be well sifted to remove all the fine particles. Make a small mound of mix where the trunk will sit.

1 You can repot the tree in the same container, or in a more suitable one, as we are doing. First, cover the drainage holes with mesh, held in place with wire loops like these.

5 It is important to trim the roots underneath as well, otherwise the tree will rise in its pot as it grows. Thick roots should be pruned hard back to encourage compact growth.

3 Some pots have additional small holes for tie wires. If not, you can use the drainage holes. You need at least two pieces of wire to make the tree secure until the roots have re-established.

4 Cover the floor of the pot with coarse grit to aid drainage. If the pot is less than 1in(2.5cm) deep you do not need a drainage course, provided the mix is sufficiently free-draining.

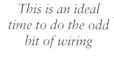

attack. The exact timing depends on the advancement of the season, geographical location and the species. Deciduous trees may start producing new roots as early as late winter, while pines may not start new root growth in earnest until mid- to late spring. The first sign of root activity is a slight swelling of the buds on last year's shoots. You can check further by gently lifting the tree from its pot and taking a close look at the roots. If the tips appear to be swelling, the time is right. If the tips are white they have already started to grow, but pruning will do them no harm so long as the new buds have not opened yet. If, on the other hand, your tree is due for repotting in theory and the buds have begun to swell but the visible roots appear brown and dead, this may be an indication of decay. You should therefore repot immediately, following the emergency steps outlined below. It is a good idea to inspect the roots of all your bonsai periodically, whether they are due for root pruning or not. This is particularly important if the tree is looking a bit off-color. As often as not, lack of vigor, wilting or premature leaf-fall is a symptom of a root-related problem, such as decay or attack by the voracious vine-weevil larva. After repotting wait two weeks before heavy pruning, and delay feeding for four to six weeks, or until new growth has been established.

1 Nestle the tree into the mound of mix, placing it just off-center for best aesthetic effect, with the surface of the root mass just below the pot's rim.

Right: *Stand the freshly repotted tree in a sheltered position until new growth starts. Do not water it again until really necessary, and do not feed it for four weeks to avoid burning the tender new roots.*

This is an ideal time to do the odd bit of wiring

Sometimes it is necessary to repot a tree 'out of season'. An emergency is likely when you inspect the roots of an ailing tree and notice they are decaying, or even missing! This may be due to fungal attack, most likely resulting from poor drainage or overfeeding or to a subterranean pest. In either instance, take the following action. Defoliate all deciduous trees to reduce water loss, and very gently comb away all the dead roots and soil. Then hose away all the remaining soil. Inspect what is left and remove any larvae and remaining dead roots. Do not cut any living roots. Plant the tree straight away in an oversized container, using a potting mix of at least 80 percent grit but no loam. Bury the roots deeper than before and water the tree, using a solution of systemic fungicide. Place the tree in an 'intensive care unit' – either a humid but ventilated polytunnel, or a plastic tent – and spray it at least once a day. Maintain an evenly damp soil. There should be just enough moisture to satisfy the tree's reduced needs but little enough to encourage the roots to grow in search of more. Using the extra gritty mix helps achieve this balance. Do not feed the tree again until it has fully recovered.

2 Next, pull the wire ties down over the root mass and twist them together until the tree does not rock. Cushion the bark with squares of rubber or foam.

3 Fill the remaining spaces with fresh potting mix. If the mix is virtually dry it is a lot easier to apply, because it runs freely and does not compact as you work it into the empty spaces.

Note how last year's shoots have been pruned to an outward facing bud.

4 Work the mix in between the roots, ensuring that there are no air pockets. Traditionalists recommend using a chopstick, but fingers are more sensitive and nearer to hand.

5 Water the newly potted tree well, using a fine rose or spray so that you do not wash away the new mix. Repeat the operation a few minutes later to ensure a thorough soaking.

Shaping with wire

Wiring is the most fundamental process in bonsai training, allowing the accurate positioning of branches and shoots. The principle is simple, but acquiring the skill takes a little time. Suitable gauge wire is coiled around a branch or shoot. When the two are bent and maneuvered into the desired position, the wire holds the branch in place. After a period of growth, the branch sets in that position and you can remove the wire (page 97). The time taken for this to happen varies from one species to another. Some deciduous species may set in a a few weeks, but conifers, especially junipers, may take several years to set, during which time you may need to remove and reapply the wire several times to avoid damaging the bark. Older, stiffer branches will also take longer, and you may have to bend them little by little every few weeks until you achieve the desired position. Every plant is an individual, and with experience you will learn just how far you can go before snapping the branch, so take it easy at first. Practice the technique on a twig or branch from a garden shrub, preferably a species similar to the one you have chosen for your bonsai. See how thick the wire needs to be, and how far the branch will bend without breaking. Custom-made aluminum wire is available from all bonsai outlets and by mail order. It is anodized to give it an unobtrusive brown finish, and although it is suitable for most purposes it can be expensive. (Here, we have used silver aluminum wire, because it shows up better in the photographs.)

The Japanese traditionally use copper wire for conifers because its superior holding power is more effective on their springier branches. If you use aluminum wire, it needs to be much thicker and is therefore more unsightly. Plastic-coated iron wire is sold in two thicknesses in garden centers and can be used as a last resort, but is too stiff and thus more difficult to apply safely. What is more, if this wire is used on junipers

Above: The branches on this old 'shimpaku' juniper from Japan were wired into position years ago, while they were young and flexible.

2 When you bend the branch, do it gradually. Spread your hands so that you are holding as much of the branch as possible and use both thumbs as leverage points.

3 Once bent, the wire should hold the branch in position. If the branch springs back, the wire is too thin, if it cuts the bark, it is too tight.

1 For your first try, use fairly thick wire which is easier to handle. Always hold the wired part of the branch firmly with one hand and coil the wire with the other.

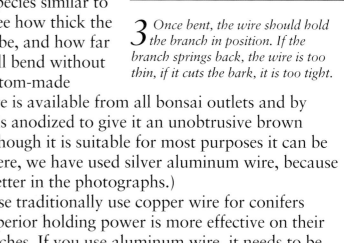

4 When wiring long branches, reduce the thickness of the wire as the branch diameter decreases. Overlap the different thicknesses by two or three turns.

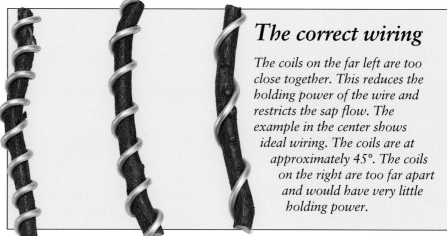

The correct wiring

The coils on the far left are too close together. This reduces the holding power of the wire and restricts the sap flow. The example in the center shows ideal wiring. The coils are at approximately 45°. The coils on the right are too far apart and would have very little holding power.

5 When wiring a side branch, anchor the wire by coiling it around the trunk. Always take it through the fork of the branch as shown.

6 The best plan is to use one piece of wire for two branches, which provides perfect anchorage. Coil the wire in the directions shown here.

7 It is also best to use one piece of wire for forked branches. Make sure you coil it in opposite directions on each branch, otherwise the wire on the first branch will uncoil as you work on the second one.

95

and the plastic coating splits, bringing the metal into contact with broken bark, it can react with cambium, turning it into a black, decaying mess, and causing the branch to die back. If allowed to remain on the branch for more than a week or two, the tree might even die.

With a little experience you will be able to assess what gauge of wire is needed for any given branch. You may need two pieces of wire for heavy branches, but this will only increase the holding power by about half. Doubling the thickness will increase the holding power by a factor of three. Plan your wiring 'strategy'. Decide where to begin and end, and cut a piece at least a third longer than the length of the branch. If you plan to use twin wires use one piece doubled up. Start by anchoring the end where the pieces are joined and work them together along the branch. If you are unhappy with your first attempt, cut off the wire and try again.

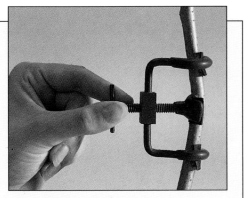

Clamps

Sometimes you may want to create a sharp bend or alter the direction of a really thick branch or trunk, where no amount of wire would have any effect. In such cases you can use a special clamp like this. Clamps are available in a variety of sizes, the largest one being capable of bending a conifer branch over 1in(2.5cm) thick.

Take care to cushion the bark against the considerable pressure applied by the clamp. Avoid trying to create too severe a bend in one go; it is much better to give the clamp an extra turn every week or so until the branch achieves the desired position.

1 A plan view of a fully wired deciduous branch. Note how the side branches are fanned out like spread fingers, and how straight lines have been avoided.

2 A side view of the same branch. It is important to build height on the branches of deciduous trees, as well as width. There is plenty of space between each shoot for future growth.

3 Pine branches are wired to a different shape. The side branches should cascade slightly from the main limb, forming a low dome. The tip of each shoot is wired to point upwards.

4 *A plan view of a juniper branch, shaped in the traditional way for the formal upright style. Note the triangular shape and how the side branches are positioned alternately.*

On junipers and pines, stripping old foliage like this allows light to stimulate back budding. For some curious reason, the wire itself also seems to have a similar affect.

Removing the wire

Wire can be expensive, so it is tempting to unwind it once it has served its purpose in order to use it another time. However, this is a risky business since it is much easier to damage the bark, or even snap the branch, when working in reverse. The branch will have swollen so the wire will be tighter than when you first applied it, and will naturally be full of kinks, making it difficult to manipulate.

It is much safer to snip the wire away using wire cutters, which cut right up to the tip of the jaws. Custom-made Japanese bonsai wire cutters are designed for this purpose, but can be quite expensive. To start with, good-quality electrical wire cutters will do the job as well if you choose the tool carefully. You will need the long-handled type to enable you to reach awkward places. Any damage to the bark caused by the cutters will be superficial and will heal much quicker than damage caused through careless uncoiling.

If you are worried about the unnecessary expense of 'wasting' wire in this way, ask yourself this question: what is the most valuable to you, a few lengths of wire or a developing bonsai that you have labored over for hours and carefully nurtured for years?

5 *If the wire stays on too long it will cut right into the bark like this. Remove it in good time and, if the branch has not set, rewire it, coiling in the opposite direction.*

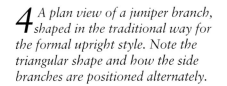

97

Branch pruning

When a branch is pruned, it inevitably leaves a scar. With full-sized trees the wound normally heals rapidly and any disfiguration will be of little or no consequence. However, since bonsai grow more slowly, the healing process is also slower and needs some help. Take great care to minimize the possibility of unsightly swellings around the wound, and to encourage the scar to blend in with the character of the trunk. Here we show how to execute simple pruning and how to turn a larger wound into an interesting feature. There are a few general points to bear in mind when pruning. Always use very sharp tools, and sterilize them, if possible, by immersing them in methylated spirit for a few minutes. This is vital when pruning away diseased wood. Seal the cambium layer (between the bark and the heartwood) against frost, water and drying wind. If left exposed it may die back, increasing the size of the wound and delaying the healing process. Never use horticultural bitumen-based sealants, as they dry hard and are impossible to remove from the surrounding bark without causing disfiguration. Feed the tree well after drastic pruning to speed up the healing process. The more vigorous the tree, the quicker it will heal. Rub off any unwanted shoots that arise around the wound as soon as they appear. Failure to do this will result in swellings around the scar, causing even more disfiguration.

1 If you do not have any bonsai tools, sharp secateurs will do. Use the 'bypass' type rather than the 'anvil' type, and make sure the non-cutting blade is furthest from the trunk.

2 Leave a small stub at first, rather than attempting to cut right up to the trunk. It is so easy to damage the bark on the trunk if you are too impatient.

3 If you do have special branch pruners, use them to finish off the cut as close to the trunk as possible. It will heal more neatly if you create a slight hollow in the exposed wood.

Disguising large wounds

Sometimes it is necessary to prune away really heavy branches, causing scars that would normally take many years to heal. Even then, they might be too large in proportion to the rest of the bonsai. However, you can turn these large scars to advantage by hollowing out the wound, through to the heartwood. If done with care, this can result in a natural-looking feature that adds age and character to the trunk. You can make the hollow as deep as you like, since the heart-wood is essentially dead, so long as the sapwood and cambium are intact.

Above: *You need to use very sharp gouges or routers when carving.*
Right: *This hollow trunk has acquired all the character of an ancient tree.*

While developing this English elm bonsai, it was necessary to prune a branch in the front of the trunk. Avoid this practice if at all possible, as the scar will be in the most noticeable place of all. However, after six or seven years the wound has healed over nicely and is beginning to blend with the surrounding bark.

4 Clean up the edges of the wound with a very sharp knife. Ragged edges heal unevenly and are likely to harbor fungal spores that may later infect the whole tree.

5 Seal the wound thoroughly, especially around the edges. If you do not have any special bonsai sealant, try mixing a little olive oil with grafting wax or children's modeling clay.

Maintenance pruning

Each year, a bonsai will throw out new shoots from the buds created in the leaf axils during the previous growing season. It only takes a few weeks for these shoots to outgrow the design of the tree and make it look very untidy. In a semi-mature or developing bonsai, you can allow these shoots to grow to six or seven leaves before cutting them back. Allowing them this period of free growth thickens the parent branches and trunk and builds up a general vigor in the tree. However, if allowed to grow too long, they will sap the strength from the finer growth and quickly kill it off. New shoots will emerge from the buds in the remaining leaf axils. At this stage, wire in any wayward shoots or those destined to become new branches. However, in established bonsai, you must cut back this annual growth during the dormant season to allow the next season's growth room to extend before outgrowing the design. Over the seasons, this constant 'clip-and-grow' technique will reward you with a much-forked branch structure, with all the characteristics of an ancient tree. Here we show how to approach the winter pruning of trees with alternate and opposite leaves. Always prune to a bud that points in the direction you want the new growth to take. If you have the patience, it is possible to style a bonsai entirely by pruning. The best time to do your winter pruning is late in the season, before the buds swell.

Above: It takes many hours each winter to carry out maintenance pruning on this trident maple to keep the fine twig structure.

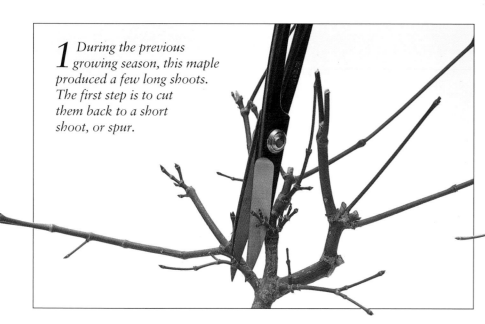

1 *During the previous growing season, this maple produced a few long shoots. The first step is to cut them back to a short shoot, or spur.*

2 *Every few years it is necessary to prune away older growth to prevent overcrowding and to maintain neat foliage pads.*

5 *Like the maple, this elm has produced some long shoots that need to be pruned first.*

6 *Unwanted shoots arising from older wood should also be cut off. Notice the stage of bud development. This is an ideal time for maintenance pruning, since you can easily see where all the tiny buds are located.*

3 *Finally, cut back all spurs to one or two buds. You may have to look quite closely to see the buds because they can be very small. Examine the base of each spur.*

4 *After a good prune, the branch looks rather naked, but remember that every remaining bud will generate a new shoot next season, producing an ever-more-compact twig structure.*

7 *This is also a good time to prune off any stubs and dead shoots. Note how each shoot has been pruned to a bud facing in the direction the new growth is required.*

8 *Each of the remaining shortened shoots bears dormant buds around the base that will sprout in the future, thus ensuring a never-ending supply of new shoots. These will eventually grow and replace the shoots you see here, which will in turn be pruned away. And so the cycle continues.*

101

Summer pinching

Once the branch structure has become established, enough new shoots should appear each spring, bearing sufficient foliage to sustain the tree without necessarily allowing any extension growth. This draws the energy from the rest of the tree, concentrating it in the growing tips, and starving the fine inner twigs of nutrients. The additional foliage prevents them gaining adequate light. The result is that the fine twigs die and the whole twig development process will need to be started again. The first step is to build and refine this tracery of fine twigs. Once this has been done, keep the resulting foliage pads trimmed and in balance with the design. You can achieve both these ends by pinching out the tips of all new growth as it appears. Different species grow in different ways, and the following techniques have been developed to accommodate the five most common growth patterns. With broadleaved trees, new shoots will emerge from the buds in the remaining leaf axils. In pines, new buds will form at the point at which the shoot is pinched, as well as further back on older growth. Larch and spruce will only produce new shoots from buds that are already visible on the remaining shoot or from around the base of the shoot and on older growth. Junipers will throw out new growth from any branch or shoot that bears foliage, and need constant pinching throughout the growing season.

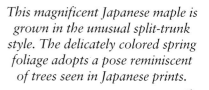

This magnificent Japanese maple is grown in the unusual split-trunk style. The delicately colored spring foliage adopts a pose reminiscent of trees seen in Japanese prints.

1 Spruce buds open to form tiny, bright green tufts that should be plucked before they have fully elongated. Do not do the whole tree at one go; spread the job over two weeks.

2 As pine buds begin to grow they elongate, forming 'candles'. Snap off up to two-thirds of this growth before the needles develop. Twist and bend it at the same time.

3 *Junipers produce prolific new growth, forming tightly packed foliage. This extension growth is distinguished by its lighter color. Hold the fan of foliage in one hand and pull out all extending growth with the finger and thumb of the other. With practice, you will be able to pinch quite large bunches of foliage in one go.*

4 *Zelkovas and other alternate-leaved species produce new leaves one at a time at the shoot tips. This leaf, and the tiny bud at its base, should be pinched out, using tweezers if necessary.*

5 *Maples produce new leaves in pairs, borne on a short extending shoot. Both leaves should be pinched out, together with the tiny developing bud nestling between them.*

Leaf pruning

Leaf pruning, the ultimate refinement technique, is only suitable for broadleaved deciduous species. It results in a very fine, compact twig formation, tiny leaves and enhanced fall color in the year it is applied. Since it causes the tree a certain amount of stress, it should only be carried out every three years or so, and only on healthy, vigorous trees. It is normally restricted to bonsai that are being prepared for exhibition. The ideal time for leaf pruning is early summer, as soon as the spring growth has hardened. The principle is similar to shoot pruning and pinching, in that reducing the foliage encourages new side growth to develop. But because the foliage is totally removed, the tree undergoes a 'false fall' and the following year's growth develops in the current year. This means that there will many more new shoots than before, bearing correspondingly more leaves. As the tree can only support – and only requires – a fixed volume of foliage, these leaves will be greatly reduced in size. Also, since these leaves only have half a season to live, they will be in better condition come the fall, resulting in brighter color over a longer period.

1 This shohin field maple received a merit award from the president of the World Bonsai Federation. Being small, it needs regular leaf pruning to reduce the scale of the leaves.

2 Even though it may seem a little unnerving at first, take the plunge and start snipping off all the leaves, one by one.

3 Cut just below the leaf, leaving the petiole, or leaf stalk, intact. This prevents excessive 'bleeding'.

4 Leaf pruning also presents an ideal opportunity to *check the progress of the branch structure. The petioles that remain on the tree will fall as soon as the new leaves start to emerge.*

5 After a week or two, *the new crop of leaves emerges, brighter and even more colorful than in the first flush of spring.*

6 Less than a month later, *the tree has grown a full crop of small brightly colored leaves, borne on short shoots.*

105

Watering and feeding

In theory, provided your bonsai is growing in a free-draining potting mix, it should not be possible to overwater it. But in their enthusiasm, many beginners manage to do just that. Over-watering eliminates the air contained in the spaces between the soil particles and 'drowns' the roots. It also creates the conditions favored by various root-rotting fungi. The symptoms of decaying roots (yellowing foliage and lack of new growth) are not usually apparent until the damage has been done. However, it does take a few weeks for the problem to become serious, so the occasional drenching will not hurt. On the other hand, it may only take 24 hours for a bonsai to die of thirst, so it is essential to prevent the soil drying out completely. Generally, the best method is to water the surface evenly, using a fine rose or spray, until water drains out of the drainage holes. Wait a few minutes and repeat. This ensures a thorough wetting of the soil and should be sufficient for one day during the height of summer. Try to avoid watering a tree that does not really need it. Even if the soil surface appears to have dried out, deeper in the pot it may still be quite wet. If in doubt, scrape away the surface in a couple of places and adjust the amount of water accordingly. The best time to water is in early evening, giving the tree plenty of time for a good drink before morning. If you cannot avoid watering in the morning, do it as early as possible. Another advantage of evening watering is that you can douse the foliage at the same time without the risk of leaf scorch caused by the water droplets acting as miniature magnifying glasses in the sun. All bonsai appreciate a daily shower.

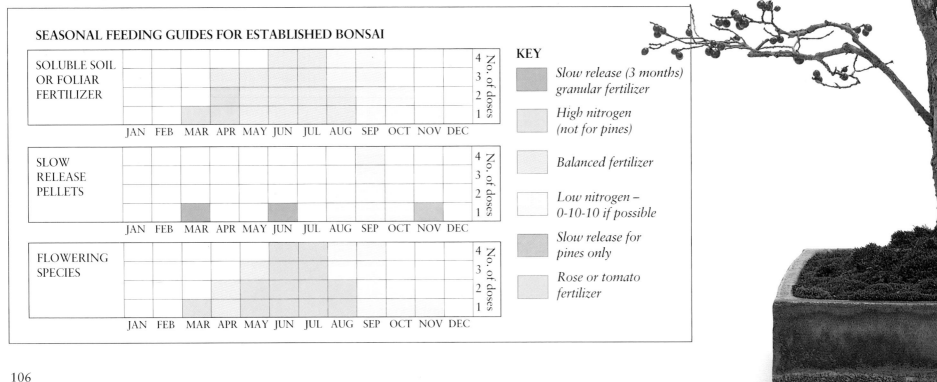

SEASONAL FEEDING GUIDES FOR ESTABLISHED BONSAI

SOLUBLE SOIL OR FOLIAR FERTILIZER — No. of doses 4 3 2 1 — JAN FEB MAR APR MAY JUN JUL AUG SEP OCT NOV DEC

SLOW RELEASE PELLETS — No. of doses 4 3 2 1 — JAN FEB MAR APR MAY JUN JUL AUG SEP OCT NOV DEC

FLOWERING SPECIES — No. of doses 4 3 2 1 — JAN FEB MAR APR MAY JUN JUL AUG SEP OCT NOV DEC

KEY

Slow release (3 months) granular fertilizer

High nitrogen (not for pines)

Balanced fertilizer

Low nitrogen – 0-10-10 if possible

Slow release for pines only

Rose or tomato fertilizer

Feeding can be a source of much confusion for the novice but the principle is really quite simple. There are three ways to apply fertilizer: by placing pellets on or in the soil, by watering it onto the soil and by spraying it on the leaves (foliar feeding). Each has advantages and disadvantages and the choice is really based on your own preference. Specialist bonsai fertilizer pellets are available from all nurseries. They can be either the organic variety, such as rape seed cake, or inorganic. Inorganic pellets are coated in a porous membrane that allows the nutrients to pass by the process of osmosis. Both types release nutrients slowly, which means that you do not have to worry about feeding for a while. The disadvantage is that you will not be able to adjust the feeding pattern without risking overfeeding, which may 'burn' the roots. There are a large number of soluble fertilizers available in garden centers and florists, most of which are suitable. (Avoid using any specifically intended for houseplants as they tend to be too rich for trees.) These can be routinely applied once a week or, better still, at a quarter strength with every watering. Always follow the manufacturer's instructions and never use a stronger solution than stated.

It is a good idea to change brand every now and then, in order to maintain a balanced diet. The disadvantage here is that the nutrients wash out of the soil quickly, so you have to be quite strict in your feeding regime. Research has shown that a plant can absorb more nutrients through it leaves than through its roots. Many standard soluble fertilizers can be applied in this way, as well as via the soil, while some are specifically designed to be applied in this manner. This technique is particularly useful when your bonsai has root problems or if the potting mixture is too wet. Foliar feeds are easy to apply, provided you do not do so in strong sun, otherwise the leaves may scorch. The only disadvantage is that in warm, windy weather the solution dries on the leaves too quickly and leaves a powdery deposit that is difficult to wash off.

Any of these methods of feeding are suitable for keeping an established tree in good health and vigor, but occasionally you may need to use a specialist feed in order to encourage the tree to perform in a specific way. Before you attempt this you will need to understand a little more about how each of the major nutrients affects the tree.

This unusual and desirable clump style bonsai is Japanese holly, or Ilex serrata. (The Japanese call it English holly!) It is encouraged to flower and fruit prolifically by a high-potassium diet.

What is NPK?

The letters NPK appear on the packs of all good-quality fertilizers and are followed by a sequence of numbers, for example, NPK7: 11 : 9.5. The letters are the chemical symbols for the three major nutrients and the numbers denote their ratio. The higher the numbers, the stronger the fertilizer. For bonsai, it is best to stick with brands with the weaker concentrations. So our example has seven parts of nitrogen (N), eleven parts of phosphorus (P) and nine-and-a-half parts of potassium (K). It represents a fairly well-balanced feed for sustaining healthy growth.

Nitrogen (N) is responsible for leaf and stem growth and can enrich the color of the foliage. Without any nitrogen, a plant would only produce a few stunted leaves and growth would be poor. The plant's health would quickly deteriorate because it would not be able to carry out the process of photosynthesis efficiently. Too much nitrogen and the growth will be too vigorous. Large leaves will be borne on long, sappy shoots that will soon outgrow their own strength, and the tree will be prone to disease. Nitrogen should be increased when you want a plant to put on a spurt of rapid growth. This applies to young, developing plants that need to grow larger before you can start to train them. If the foliage is dull (not yellow, which indicates a root problem) a little extra nitrogen may improve the color. Apply a high-nitrogen feed as the tree needs it, not before. In spring, after growth has started, or once new leaves have emerged following leaf pruning, an application of a high-nitrogen feed will replenish the tree's resources.

Phosphorus (P) is primarily responsible for root growth. It also encourages thick, sturdy trunks, helps to strengthen the plant against disease and frosts, and promotes back-budding. An excess may result in poor foliage growth and color. Phosphorus is especially useful after repotting or when a tree is recovering from a root problem, so you can apply a little extra at such times. In fact, a high-phosphorus and potassium feed will aid recovery from many ailments. Increasing the phosphorus content in the diet in late summer and fall toughens up the tree in readiness for the fall. A pinch of powdered superphosphate on the surface of the soil is an easy method of application.

Korean hornbeams naturally develop this attractive streaky bark, even in young trees.

Potassium (K), or potash, is responsible for encouraging flowers and fruit as well as hardening off late growth before the winter. If left out of its diet, a plant will fail to flower. Even if it does flower, the blooms will be of poor quality and the fruit will not set. Potassium also helps to build up resistance to disease.

From what we have learned above, it is easy to deduce how to use each element to produce specific results by increasing its proportion in the fertilizer. Here are some pointers as to why and when this should be done. Potassium should be increased for all flowering and fruiting bonsai. A diluted rose or tomato feed is ideal, as these are specifically formulated to increase the flowering and fruiting potential. Potash can also be increased to help weak plants regain strength. Extra potassium given during late summer and fall will help the tree combat the perils of winter. A little sulfate of potash sprinkled on the soil once a week will do the trick.

A spacing bar is used to hold two trunks apart until they are set in the desired position.

Some nurseries sell a specialist soluble fertilizer called '0-10-10' which, as the name implies, is nitrogen-free and is ideal for late-season feeding. When buying fertilizers, make sure that they include trace elements. These are only required in minute quantities but without them your bonsai will surely suffer. If you do use products that do not contain trace elements you should add them separately twice a year.

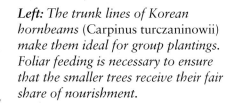

Left: *The trunk lines of Korean hornbeams (Carpinus turczaninowii) make them ideal for group plantings. Foliar feeding is necessary to ensure that the smaller trees receive their fair share of nourishment.*

Right: *Organic fertilizer pellets can be either evenly distributed on the surface, or lightly pressed into the soil. They break down with watering and release the nutrients gradually over a three month period.*

This wavy trunk line results from hard pruning the stem of a plant with alternate leaves.

Right: *Foliar feed can be applied either with a hand spray or a watering can. A spray allows localized feeding of weaker branches, in order to build up their strength.*

109

Part Five

GROWING ORCHIDS

Orchids have been popular in cultivation for nearly 200 years, ever since the first exotic specimens arrived in Europe from the newly explored tropical and subtropical regions. They are one of the most successful plant families and grow on every landmass, from the equator to the very edge of the Arctic Circle. In the tropical zones they have reached their zenith, with flamboyant blooms of incredible richness and variety. These are the epiphytes, or air plants, that grow on trees but are not parasitic. Most of the epiphytes produce swollen stems known as pseudobulbs that hold reserves of water for the plant and also support the leaves and roots. Roots are often exposed to absorb moisture from the air. In the cooler, temperate zones, orchids grow in the ground as terrestrials, producing rosettes of leaves and blooms from the center.

Orchid plants may be sympodial, meaning that each season they produce either independent flowering growths or pseudobulbs from a horizontal rhizome. Cymbidiums, for example, produce pseudobulbs, while paphiopedilums produce growths. Others have a monopodial system and produce a vertical rhizome from which new leaves grow from the center. Vandas, for example, have long rhizomes and phalaenopsis have short ones. Orchid blooms are unique and incredibly diverse. All have three sepals, which resemble the petals, and three petals. One petal, called the lip, is different and is designed to attract pollinating insects. A single central structure, the column, contains the male and female parts fused together and hidden from view.

This section looks at some popular orchids and how to grow them. As an introduction to their enchanted world, we hope that it will stimulate you to look more closely at these fascinating plants.

Left: Vanda *Rothschildiana, a famous old hybrid.* **Right:** *Orchids are striking and unusual in shape and color.*

111

Cymbidiums

Cymbidiums are the most widely grown orchids. Their well-deserved popularity stems from their ease of growth and the wonderful range of hybrids available in all colors, from white and cream to yellow and green, and from pink to red and bronze. Their flowering season extends from late fall throughout the winter and spring to the late-blooming types in early summer. From a collection of mixed hybrids you can expect to have blooms for almost nine months of the year, and these blooms will last for a good eight to ten weeks. The flower spikes are usually taller than the foliage and may be upright, arching or pendent in their habit. The plants produce rounded pseudobulbs that may be the size of an egg or as large as a tennis ball. Each supports eight to ten narrow leaves, which may be 18-24in(45-60cm) long. They produce vigorous, thick and fleshy roots.

Most of the species that have been used to create the modern hybrids come from the Himalayas in India, with a few others from Burma, Vietnam, Taiwan, China and parts of Australia. These species include *Cymbidium lowianum, insigne, traceyanum, pumilum* and *devonianum*. The cymbidium species themselves are not so generally grown and are usually confined to specialist collections.

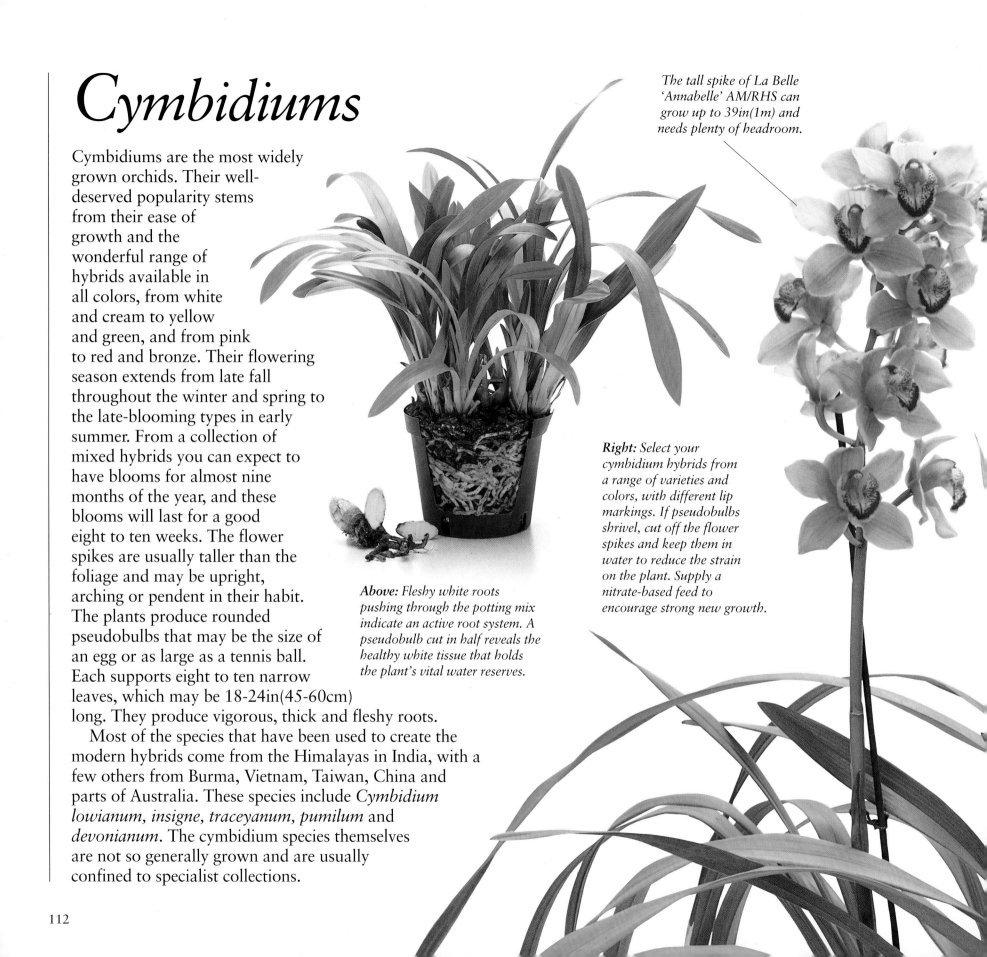

The tall spike of La Belle 'Annabelle' AM/RHS can grow up to 39in(1m) and needs plenty of headroom.

Above: *Fleshy white roots pushing through the potting mix indicate an active root system. A pseudobulb cut in half reveals the healthy white tissue that holds the plant's vital water reserves.*

Right: *Select your cymbidium hybrids from a range of varieties and colors, with different lip markings. If pseudobulbs shrivel, cut off the flower spikes and keep them in water to reduce the strain on the plant. Supply a nitrate-based feed to encourage strong new growth.*

York 'Ever Blooming' is an older cymbidium variety, but still very popular with growers today.

The parents of this new top-quality variety are Quetivel Mill and Granos Vaux.

Jessie 'Blakistone' is typical of the miniature varieties that are highly suitable for growing indoors.

Cooksbridge 'Pinkie' is another successful hybrid. It has attractive, delicate pastel coloring.

Basically, there are two groups of cymbidium hybrids to choose from: the miniatures and the standards. The miniature varieties have come later to prominence but excel over the standards because they are more compact, bloom more freely, are less demanding of light and carry more blooms per flower spike. This makes them better suited to growing indoors, where so many of them are now seen. Their blooms can be 2-3in(5-7.5cm) across the petals.

The standard varieties are bigger all round, with blooms up to 5in(13cm) across. Adult plants can become exceedingly large and difficult to handle, requiring pots of 12in(30cm) or more in diameter. However, a fine, well-grown plant of this size with six or more 36in(90cm) flower spikes in full bloom is quite breathtaking, and hard to beat. If you have the space and headroom in a greenhouse or sunroom, think big!

Growing cymbidiums

Cymbidiums are cool growing, so provide them with a temperature no less than 50°F(10°C) on winter nights, rising by 10-15°F(5-8°C) during the day. Lower temperatures than this will restrict their growth and affect their flowering, as will much higher levels at night. The summer temperature should not exceed 85°F(30°C) by day. Higher temperatures will stress the plants and cause premature leaf loss, again affecting their flowering. Shade cymbidiums from direct sunshine throughout the summer and give as much light as possible during the winter. Wherever practical, grow cymbidiums outdoors in summer. Water plants all year round, and feed in spring, summer and fall. Spray the leaves daily in summer.

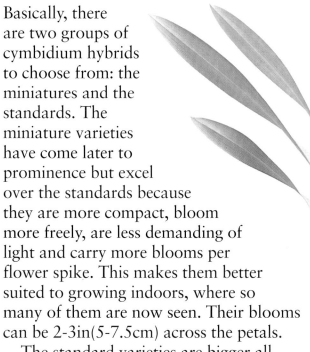

Below: Cymbidium madidum *is an unusual variety from Australia.*

Cymbidium madidum *has been used successfully to produce some delightful yellow hybrids.*

GROWING CYMBIDIUMS

Seasonal activity
Plants grow nearly all year. Flowering period winter to early summer. Evergreen.

Location
Greenhouse or sunroom in winter. Keep outside in summer if possible. Miniatures will grow indoors.

Temperature
Summer maximum: 85°F(30°C)
Winter day: 60-65°F(16-18°C)
Night minimum: 50°F(10°C)

Light/Shade
Shade from direct sunshine in summer, provide maximum light in winter.

Watering/Spraying
Water all year round. Spray leaves daily in summer.

Feeding
Spring, summer and fall.

Right: This example of the hybridizer's art shows the Indian species Cymbidium devonianum *(left) with one of its hybrids, Sea Jade 'Freshwater' AM/RHS.*

Both C. madidum *and* C. devonianum *produce pendent flower spikes, a reminder that these epiphytic orchids grow on trees in the wild.*

Odontoglossums & Miltoniopsis

Any of the orchids within this group are ideal for the beginner and make good subjects for growing indoors, in a sunroom or in a greenhouse. What is more, they include the most gaily colored flowers of all the orchids. Odontoglossum blooms are uniquely patterned, with individual designs to a degree that no other orchid has achieved. Their pseudobulbs are oval, from light to dark green, with four narrowly oval leaves, the center pair being 6-9in(15-23cm) long. They have an abundance of fine roots. Miltoniopsis are similar, but carry five leaves, their paler coloring matching that of the pseudobulbs. Only a few of the species within these groups are available to growers due to their scarcity. The hybrids offer a far wider range of colors, as well as being more robust and therefore easier to grow. Much interbreeding with additional, closely allied genera within this group, including *Cochlioda*, *Oncidium* and *Brassia*, has produced the intergeneric hybrids that have given rise to the fantastic variety now available. The most popular genera are *Odontioda (Odontoglossum x Cochlioda)*, *Odontonia (Odontoglossum x Miltoniopsis)*, *Odontocidium (Odontoglossum x Oncidium)*, *Vuylstekeara (Miltoniopsis x Odontioda)* and *Wilsonara (Odontioda x Oncidium)*. Further man-made genera within this group become considerably complex and all are loosely referred to as odontoglossum types. These hybrids can be traced back to the original South American species, most of which come from high elevations in the Andes. Their range extends from Mexico, through Colombia, crossing the equator to Peru.

This cutaway view of the pot reveals the healthy root system, with live roots actively progressing through the potting mix.

A clone of Odontioda La Hougie Bie.

Vuylstekeara *Cambria 'Plush' FCC/RHS is one of the most popular varieties today. Note the large, flared lip, which has come from crossing with Miltoniopsis.*

Above: *A mature odontoglossum can be comfortably accommodated in a 5in(13cm) pot. This is a healthy plant, with good color to its foliage. All its pseudobulbs are in leaf. Strong new growth is developing well at the front of the plant and this will develop into the next flowering pseudobulb.*

Right: *This selection of modern hybrids shows odontoglossums, odontiodas and a Vuylstekeara. Selective breeding for over 100 years has created the range of colors and contributed to the variety in size and shape of blooms.*

Odontioda *Marie Noel, a top-quality variety.*

Note the superb rounded shape of this fine example of Odontioda *Aloette x Flocalo.*

The species Odontoglossum crispum *has been involved in the breeding of all the plants shown on this page.*

The rich color of Odontioda *Marie Noel originated from the red* Cochlioda noezliana.

Odontioda *La Hougie Bie is a lovely yellow hybrid.*

Odontoglossum *Augres extends the variation in color combinations.*

Because of their involved breeding, these hybrids do not have specific flowering times. Mostly, they bloom as their latest pseudobulb nears completion at the end of the growing cycle. Vuylstekearas will regularly bloom approximately every nine months. The miltoniopsis, being less interbred, will have their main flowering in early summer, with a secondary display in the fall. However, the quality of the blooms may not be of the same standard on the second flowering, or when they bloom in the heat of the summer. They should last in perfection for up to six weeks.

Growing odontoglossums and miltoniopsis

Keep these orchids out of the direct sun and well shaded during the summer. An advantage of indoor growing is less temperature fluctuation, but avoid overheating in the summer. If temperatures exceed 80°F(27°F) for long periods during the day, either find a cooler place indoors – such as a window that does not receive sunlight – or move odontoglossums outside for the summer months. Miltoniopsis leaves are too soft for these orchids to be summered out of doors. If odontoglossums and miltoniopsis are subjected to very high temperatures, the stress can cause premature loss of leaves and possibly roots, as well as checking growth. The winter night temperatures should be no lower than 54°F(12°C).

Odontoglossum types and miltoniopsis can be watered throughout the year, always keeping the plants moist enough to maintain plump pseudobulbs. These will quickly shrivel if allowed to become overdry. At the same time, be sure to give them plenty of fresh air. Feeding can be all year round, giving less in winter, more in summer. Spray odontoglossums lightly in summer, but keep the leaves of miltoniopsis plants dry.

Left: Two young plants of identical age. The one on the left is flowering, delaying the start of the new growth. On the right, new growth is well advanced. Miltoniopsis do not normally grow and flower at the same time.

Right: A group of very colorful hybrids featuring the predominant colors in this genus. Their main flowering season is early summer and they have the added bonus of fragrant blooms.

This new hybrid is a cross between Woodlands 'Alba' and Charlesworthii, two very old plants.

GROWING ODONTOGLOSSUMS AND MILTONIOPSIS

Seasonal activity
Plants grow nearly all year. Flowering period varies according to type. Evergreen.

Location
Indoors, greenhouse or sunroom. Odontoglossums can be kept outside in summer.

Temperature
Summer maximum: 80°F(27°C)
Winter day: 60-65°F(16-18°C)
Night minimum: 54°F(12°C)

Light/Shade
Shade from direct sunshine in summer.

Watering/Spraying
Water all year round. Keep plants moist. Spray odontoglossums lightly in summer, but keep miltoniopsis leaves dry.

Feeding
All year, more in summer, less in winter.

This very fine hybrid is a top variety produced in France and called Anjou 'St. Patrick'.

The darkest red is captured in the rich tones of the German-bred Hamburg 'The King'.

This is a lovely hybrid raised in the USA, called Rouge 'California Plum'.

This is 'Arctic Moon', one of the forms of the Colombian species, Miltoniopsis vexillaria, *which produced these hybrids.*

Phalaenopsis

The popularity of phalaenopsis has increased in recent years as they are easy to grow and bloom indoors, and can produce flowers all year round. An average plant will carry three to five 6in(15cm) leaves at any time. These are roundly oval, thick and fleshy and often glossy. New leaves grow from a central rhizome, without pseudobulbs. Among the orchids they are noted for their very beautiful roots, which often grow outside the pot, adhering to any surface that they touch. They are silvery-gray and flattened, with delicate pink or green growing tips. Always take care not to snap these off.

The flower spike comes from near the base, usually following the formation of a leaf.

It is quite usual for phalaenopsis to produce their roots outside the pot. These roots are alive but inactive until green tips appear.

Above: *Phalaenopsis are monopodial orchids that grow new leaves from the tip of a vertical rhizome. An average plant has three to five leaves at any time.*

When large enough, phalaenopsis will often produce a branching flower spike, as seen here on this beautiful hybrid, Michael Davis.

As with so many of the orchids, the species are in the domain of the true collector, but a multitude of hybrids have been raised for the hobby grower and these are sufficient to satisfy the most ardent enthusiast. The main species are inhabitants of the Philippine Islands and Borneo, while others are found from Thailand to Malaysia. From the species *Phalaenopsis sanderiana*, *stuartiana* and *schilleriana* have come a host of lovely hybrids in varying shades of white and pink. With the introduction of other species, including *amboinense* and *sumatrana*, many beautiful yellow varieties have been developed. To these basic colors can be added the striped and spotted types, giving even more choice.

With phalaenopsis, flower spikes follow the growth of a new leaf and it is not unusual for more than one spike to be in bloom at any one time. Sometimes a succession of

This semi-alba variety is one of the top hybrids raised in France. It is called Plaisir de Valec.

Left: *Although their colors are limited, there is abundant variety in phalaenopsis. The plants like to be kept warm and usually do very well indoors. Their flowering season is all through the year.*

These huge, rosy pink flowers are typical of another French hybrid, known as Touraine.

Spotted varieties are very attractive, as is clear from this latest variety, which is called Babette.

Barbara Moler x Misty Green, produced along different breeding lines, is smaller in stature.

bloom is produced, extending the flowering period even further. In addition, cutting back a flower spike to a lower node will almost always create a second blooming on that spike. In this way, it is possible for a single mature plant to be in bloom for nine months at a time.

The blooms can measure up to 4in(10cm) across, the generous petals spread wide and flat, partially concealing the sepals. The lip is small and neat, either delicately marked or flushed a deeper shade.

Growing phalaenopsis

Phalaenopsis will adapt remarkably well to indoor culture, provided they are kept in a warm spot away from drafts and out of direct sunlight. In a greenhouse or sunroom, where they will mix happily with other orchids, they also require good humidity to balance a high temperature of 65°F(18°C) at night, rising by 20°F(12°C) during the day, and the normal variation between summer and winter temperatures. The plants will not die if grown at temperatures lower than those recommended, but they will not flourish so well and may be susceptible to leaf or center growth rot. A leaf can collapse and become 'watery' overnight. Indoors, you can sponge or lightly mist their leaves every day to keep them fresh and free from dust. Confine greenhouse spraying to the summer months and never make it so heavy that water runs into the center of the plants.

Water phalaenopsis all year round, keeping them evenly moist without overwatering. Encourage the growth of any roots that are overhanging the pot by spraying them. Remember that once growing in the open, the roots cannot be put back into the pot. Phalaenopsis grow all year round, albeit at a slower pace during the winter, and so you can feed them lightly all year, decreasing the frequency during the dullest winter months. Underwatering will cause dehydration and the leaves will become limp. Indoors, always keep the plants in a humidity tray with a little water just below them. In this way, they will always be near to some moisture.

Left: Phalaenopsis *Golden Emperor 'Sweet' represents the development of the smaller-flowered hybrid. There is little difference in the size of the plant, but the flower spikes are less tall and the blooms more open and of a slightly heavier texture. Yellow is the dominant color in this very attractive group of orchids, which have been bred from Malayan species.*

Right: Chamonix is typical of the large-flowered hybrids bred for many generations to obtain a perfectly round flower. Mature plants are capable of producing more flower per plant for their size than any other orchid. Sprays of a dozen or more blooms are not uncommon. These basically pink or white varieties are raised from Philippine species.

GROWING PHALAENOPSIS

Seasonal activity
Plants grow and flower all year round. Evergreen.

Location
Indoors, greenhouse or sunroom. Keep away from drafts.

Temperature
Summer maximum: 85°F(30°C)
Winter day: 75°F(24°C)
Night minimum: 65°F(18°C)

Light/Shade
Keep in shade.

Watering/Spraying
Water all year. Keep plants evenly moist. Spray exposed roots and spray plants lightly in summer.

Feeding
All year, less in winter.

Cattleyas & Vandas

These two groups contain some of the most colorful and flamboyant orchids. Indeed, their blooms are among the largest of the cultivated types.

The cattleyas make strong, robust plants with vigorous club-shaped pseudobulbs supporting one or two thickly textured leaves. These are broadly or narrowly oval, measuring up to about 6in(15cm) long. The plants have a thickened rhizome – often visible on the surface – from which the pseudobulbs grow at short, regular intervals. They produce thick, extensive roots, which can grow to a considerable length.

Because of extensive interbreeding between the related genera *Sophronitis, Laelia, Cattleya, Brassavola* and others, there are many hybrid genera in the group. These include *Sophrocattleya, Brassocattleya, Laeliocattleya* and other combinations, all of which are loosely termed cattleyas. Their flowering periods are spring or fall, with blooms lasting up to three weeks. Nearly all are fragrant to a greater or lesser degree. The species from which the modern hybrids have been produced are epiphytic plants mainly from Central and South America. A few species are still in cultivation compared with hundreds of hybrids.

Depending upon the type created by this hybridizing, the blooms may be as small as 2.5in(5cm) in the miniature varieties, to 6in(15cm) across in the standards. Colors range from pristine white, through delicate pink, purple and yellow shades to vibrant reds, oranges and even bronze. Their magnificent lips are mostly flared, frilled and richly colored in brighter hues. The buds - maybe one or two or up to six or eight - grow from the top of the pseudobulb, usually protected in their early development by a sheath, which splits as the buds emerge.

Below: Sophrolaeliocattleya *Jewel Box 'Scheherazade' AM/RHS shows off its brilliant red coloring. This superb color, together with its compact size, has come from the species* Sophronitis coccinea.

Left: Laeliocattleya *Barbara Belle 'Apricot' is a good example of the most popular type of cattleya. The large, decorative blooms are among the most flamboyant of orchids. Greenhouse or sunroom culture in good light suits them best.*

Below: Sophrolaeliocattleya *Rocket Burst 'Deep Enamel' shows considerable influence from the species* Cattleya aurantiaca, *as well as the miniature* Sophronitis coccinea. *It bears small, bright orange blooms with an exceptionally small lip.*

Below: Another small-growing group of cattleyas is represented by this Cattleya *Miva Glossa. These cattleyas are seen in delicate pastel shades, as well as in the elusive green – a color derived from C. bicolor.*

The vandas and their close allies, the ascocendas, *(Vanda x Ascocentrum)* complement the *Cattleya* groups very well and the two can be successfully grown together. The vandas are tall-growing plants that produce pairs of narrow, oval leaves from a central growing point of a vertical rhizome. Aerial roots adorn the lower portion of the rhizome, which has become devoid of foliage. The flower spikes, each usually carrying six or eight blooms, arise from the base of the leaves, mainly during the summer, and last for several weeks. Although the variety in vandas is not so great, hybrids are available in superbly rich colors, including blue, red, orange and yellow. More often these colors are enhanced by interlacing lines or tessellation (also known as marbling) on the dominant lower sepals, which are flat and rounded, dwarfing the more diminutive lip.

A small number of species, mostly from Burma, have produced the hybrids of today. The most notable of these is *Vanda coerulea*, a beautiful species with sky blue flowers. When this was crossed with *Vanda (Eulanthe) sanderiana* from the Philippines, the result was one of the most famous orchids of all time – the deep blue *Vanda Rothschildiana*, which is still the best type to grow. It readily blooms two or three times a year, a performance that most other vandas find hard to emulate. Curiously, the blooms open quite pale. The color intensifies over the first few days as the flowers mature.

GROWING CATTLEYAS

Seasonal activity
Plants grow in spring and summer. They flower in spring or fall and rest in winter. Evergreen.

Location
Greenhouse or sunroom. Miniature hybrids grow indoors.

Temperature
Summer maximum: 85°F(30°C)
Winter day: 65°F(18°C)
Night minimum: 55°F(13°C)

Light/Shade
Provide plenty of light but avoid direct sun.

Watering/Spraying
Water well in summer, very little in winter. Spray lightly in summer.

Feeding
Spring to fall.

Growing cattleyas and vandas

Cattleyas are intermediate orchids, requiring a minimum winter night temperature of 55°F(13°C) and plenty of light. Because of this light requirement, the best way to grow them is in a greenhouse or sunroom. Indoors, they can take up a lot of space and be reluctant to bloom. However, the miniature hybrids are the exception and well suited to growing indoors. Most cattleyas have a resting period during the winter, or at some other season, when they require very little water.

Because of their growing habit, vandas are cultivated in open slatted baskets and suspended by string or wire near the glass in a greenhouse or sunroom, where they will receive plenty of light. In this position, they need a regular spray at least once a day. Cattleya temperatures will suit the vandas.

Below: The most popular and free-flowering of all the vandas is Vanda Rothschildiana, *one of the finest examples of a blue orchid.*

Cattleyas that produce a single leaf on each pseudobulb are described as unifoliate.

Note the extensive aerial roots on this vanda growing in an open basket.

GROWING VANDAS

Seasonal activity
Plants grow in spring, summer and fall. Growth slows in winter. They flower in summer. Evergreen.

Location
Suspend in slatted baskets near greenhouse or sunroom glass.

Temperature
Summer maximum: 85°F(30°C)
Winter day: 65°F(18°C)
Night minimum: 55°F(13°C

Light/Shade
Provide plenty of light but avoid direct sun.

Watering/Spraying
Water and spray at least once a day.

Feeding
Spring to fall.

Left: *This group of cattleyas and a vanda give a good indication of the habits of the plants. All these specimens are mature plants that have flowered and illustrate a typical range of sizes. A selection of these two genera will provide exotic blooms during the year. The flowers will last from three to six weeks.*

This cattleya has two leaves on each pseudobulb and belongs to the bifoliate group.

127

Zygopetalums, Masdevallias, Encyclias & Coelogynes

With so many orchids to choose from, the following is a limited selection of the more popular types. They are by no means the only ones available, merely a brief summary of some of the other varieties you can grow. They are suitable for beginners and can be kept small by dividing, if you do not want them to become too large.

Zygopetalums are handsome orchids with large pseudobulbs and four leaves. These are ribbed and narrowly oval, brittle and easily damaged. The flower spikes come from inside the first leaf on the partially completed pseudobulb and usually produce six to eight flowers measuring 3in(7.5cm) across, in a rich combination of dark brown sepals and petals and indigo lips. This is the basic coloring for hybrids produced from the Brazilian species *Zygopetalum mackayi*. These fall-flowering hybrids are more robust and easier to grow in a cool, shady position indoors or in a greenhouse.

Masdevallias are another extraordinary genus from South America, with a variety of species and hybrids in all sizes, ranging from less than 2in(5cm) to 6in(15cm) high. They do not have pseudobulbs and their foliage can be tufted and grasslike, while the larger species have broader leaves. The flowers are characterized by the triangular-shaped sepals, which may have long or short tails. The petals and lip are minute and almost unseen at the center of the flower. Most have single blooms on a stem, a few have more, sometimes in succession. Species and hybrids are grown along with related genera, which include draculas and dryadellas. All like cool, airy conditions with shade and this is best achieved in a greenhouse. Keep the plants evenly moist – but not too wet – all year round.

GROWING ZYGOPETALUMS

Seasonal activity
Plants grow in spring and summer. They flower in fall and rest in winter. Evergreen.

Location
Indoors or in a greenhouse.

Temperature
Summer maximum: 85°F(30°C)
Winter day: 60-65°F(16-18°C)
Night minimum: 50°F(10°C)

Light/Shade
Keep in shade.

Watering/Spraying
Water in spring, summer and fall. Do not spray.

Feeding
Spring, summer and fall.

Encyclia vitellina

Encyclia cochleata, *the cockleshell orchid.*

Masdevallia veitchiana *x Angel Frost*

Masdevallia corniculata

Masdevallia *Whiskers*

Left: *An attractive and slightly more unusual zygopetalum, known as Helen Ku. This hybrid remains small and compact, producing a limited number of blooms on the stem.*

Below: *A delightful mixed group of orchids that will add interest and color, as well as fragrance, to any collection. They are all ideal subjects for growing in a confined space.*

Encyclias (from South America) and coelogynes (from India and Malaysia) are both pretty genera containing great variety. Many are petite and ideal for indoors. Most have elongated or rounded pseudobulbs and neat foliage, and bloom during the winter, spring or early summer. The flowers of *Encyclia* grow in small clusters on upright stems from the top of the pseudobulb, while coelogyne flowers more often appear from inside the new growth. Encyclias are sometimes fragrant and their main coloring is white to creamy white, with red-lined lips. Top varieties to grow are *Encyclia pentotis* and *radiata*, but there are others that are quite different and distinct. The fragrant spring-flowering *Coelogyne ochracea*, for example, is white with yellow on the lips, while the winter-flowering *C. cristata* has large white flowers with yellow on the lips. Grow these orchids in cool conditions in good light and give them less water in winter. Do not let the pseudobulbs shrivel as a result of underwatering. Some varieties grow extremely well and are ideal for beginners.

Coelogyne ochracea

Coelogyne speciosa *var.* alba

Dryadella edwallii

Maxillaria rufescens

GROWING MASDEVALLIAS	GROWING ENCYCLIAS AND COELOGYNES
Seasonal activity Grow in summer. Flower mainly in summer. No rest period. Evergreen.	**Seasonal activity** Grow in spring and summer. Flower in winter, spring or early fall. Rest in winter. Evergreen.
Location Cool airy greenhouse.	**Location** Indoors, greenhouse, sunroom.
Temperature Summer maximum: 75°F(24°C) Winter day: 62°F(17°C) Night minimum: 52°F(11°C)	**Temperature** Summer maximum: 80°F(27°C) Winter day: 60°F(16°C) Night minimum: 50°F(10°C)
Light/Shade Provide shade.	**Light/Shade** Provide good light.
Watering/Spraying Keep moist all year round. Do not spray.	**Watering/Spraying** Water less in winter. Spray in summer.
Feeding Spring, summer and fall.	**Feeding** Spring, summer and fall.

Maxillarias, Oncidiums & Epidendrums

Maxillarias can be particularly appealing if you like small flowers on miniature plants, although some species, such as *M. sanderiana* and *grandiflora*, are really large by comparison. The smaller species are suitable for growing indoors and will bloom freely in good light. The most rewarding species are *M. tenuifolia* from Honduras, which has yellow flowers overlaid with red spotting; the summer-flowering *M. ochroleuca* from South America, which has delightful filigree flowers – white with yellow or orange lips; and the winter-flowering *M. picta* from Brazil, with yellow flowers, barred red on the outside. All are fragrant and produce their flowers singly on the stem. There are very few hybrids in this genus.

Oncidiums from Central America are popular and colorful. While the species are becoming harder to find in nurseries, a few superb hybrids have all the glamor anyone could wish for. The plants are similar in appearance to odontoglossums, to which they are related and with which they will interbreed. The typical *Oncidium* produces a tall, slender stem that branches out at the top to produce a shower of bright yellow flowers. The sepals and petals are small, but superimposed by an enlarged lip, typically measuring 1.6in(4cm) across. For best results, grow at intermediate temperatures in good light, indoors or in a greenhouse. Other species, such as *Oncidium papilio* and *luridum* from the West Indies, are representative of the warmer-growing varieties.

Epidendrums are wonderfully varied and produce some very dramatic blooms. The plants range from the diminutive *E. polybulbon* from Trinidad, to the giant *E. ibaguense* from Mexico. The latter is a reed type with long stems that produce heads of bright red flowers. On a large plant it becomes perpetually blooming. Most grow cool to intermediate and like good light with some shade.

GROWING ONCIDIUMS

Seasonal activity
Plants grow in spring and summer, flower in fall, and rest in winter. Evergreen.

Location
Indoors, greenhouse or sunroom.

Temperature
Summer maximum: 85°F(30°C)
Winter day: 65°F(18°C)
Night minimum: 55°F(13°C)

Light/Shade
Provide good light.

Watering/Spraying
Water all year, less in winter. Spray in spring and summer.

Feeding
Spring to fall.

GROWING EPIDENDRUMS

Seasonal activity
Plants grow in summer, flower in spring. Rest in winter (except miniatures).

Location
Large varieties, greenhouse or sunroom. Miniatures indoors.

Temperature
Summer maximum: 85°F(30°C)
Winter day: 65°F(18°C)
Night minimum: 55°F(13°C)

Light/Shade
Most varieties need good light.

Watering/Spraying
Water well in summer, less in winter. Spray spring and summer.

Feeding
Spring to fall.

Flower spikes will bore through the potting mix to emerge under the plant.

Above: *A stunning* Epidendrum falcatum *shows the pendent habit of the plant, which is growing on bark.*

GROWING MAXILLARIAS

Seasonal activity
Plants grow in summer. Flowering season varies according to type. Plants rest in winter. Evergreen.

Location
Smaller species are suitable for indoor growing, larger species in greenhouse or sunroom.

Temperature
Summer maximum: 85°F(30°C)
Winter day: 60°F(16°C)
Night minimum: 50°F(10°C)

Light/Shade
Provide plenty of light.

Watering/Spraying
Water all year, less in winter. Spray in summer.

Feeding
Spring, summer and fall.

Left: Oncidium maculatum *from South America is a strong, robust plant that blooms freely in the early summer. It produces short sprays of brown and buff flowers.*

Right: Maxillaria sanderiana *is one of the giants of the genus. This plant is at its best when grown in a hanging basket to show off its pendent flowers.*

These are large flowers, 3.2in(8cm) across.

Paphiopedilums

Paphiopedilums produce beautiful mottled foliage without pseudobulbs and make decorative houseplants. Their distinctly handsome flowers are borne singly on mostly tall stems, and an unusual feature is a lip modified into a pouch, which has given rise to the popular name 'lady's slipper'. Hybrids are mostly grown from species found in Burma or Thailand. Other types, defined by their plain green foliage, have heavier, more rounded flowers.

These orchids like to be warm, so provide a minimum temperature of 60°F(16°C) and moist, shady conditions. They can be watered all year round. Indoor culture suits them well and they are often seen growing alongside phalaenopsis (see page 120). The mottled-leaved varieties may flower at almost any time, but mainly during spring and summer, and the blooms will last for many weeks. The plain-leaved types are mostly winter and spring-flowering. Keep plants in as small a pot as possible, often repotting into the same size pot. Avoid getting water into the center of growths.

The dorsal sepal is a dominant feature of paphiopedilums and is usually flared or spotted.

The main feature is the pouch, which is a modified lip. There is little variation in the basic shape.

The petals may be short, narrow or wide, depending on the variety. In some cases, they may be exceptionally long, horizontal or drooping.

Left: This is a German-bred hybrid, known as Celle, which represents what is now the most popular type of paphiopedilum flower. Other types have more rounded blooms.

Right: This group shows mostly mottled-leaved varieties bred from the species, Paphiopedilum callosum and its hybrid Maudiae. They are known collectively as Maudiae types.

P. lawrenceanum x *Vintners' Treasure, a tall and elegant Maudiae type.*

Some specimens of Colorado produce flowers as large as this. All are very long-lasting.

Elsie x Maudiae has a small but richly colored flower.

Gowerianum van album x William Matthews, *another variation from similar breeding lines.*

Primcolor, a charming, small-flowered variety of different breeding. The flowers are produced in succession.

Nougatine, a green-leaved variety with heavier bloom, can be traced back to the species, P. insigne.

Primulinum x Maudiae, an attractive small-flowered variety.

Aladin produces an unusual pink flower on a shorter stem.

133

Dendrobiums

Dendrobiums come from many parts of the Old World, including Australia and New Guinea. The showiest and most popular are hybrids from the Indian species, *Dendrobium nobile*. They are easy to bloom and come in a multitude of colors from white and yellow, through shades of pink and red. All have decorative lips of distinctive coloring. They produce elongated pseudobulbs – known as canes – up to 18in(45cm) tall, with leaves at right angles along their length. Flowers are produced in twos or threes along the canes between the leaves.

Dendrobiums flower in the spring after resting. Grow in cool or intermediate conditions and remember that good light is essential for flowering. Water well in summer, but keep the plants dry during the winter.

With superb amethyst and white blooms, *Ekapol* is one of the most popular of the phalaenopsis *types*.

Below: *Varieties of the* nobile *type. These hybrids are highly decorative and bloom along the length of their canes. Also illustrated are* D. infundibulum *and a similar hybrid that bloom from the top half of their canes.*

Dendrobium infundibulum *is an extremely free-flowering species from India.*

Nobile *type dendrobiums bloom from older, leafless canes. It may take two years for one cane to flower out completely.*

Left: Dendrobium *Dale Takiguchi is a phalaenopsis type, with colors from white to amethyst. Flowering stems grow from the top of long pseudobulbs.*

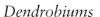

The buds and stems of
D. infundibulum *are covered
with dense black hairs. It
makes a decorative plant.*

*Dawn Marie, an unusual,
attractive hybrid,
flowers from the
top of the cane.*

*These plants can grow to a
considerable height and require
plenty of light. This* nobile *type
hybrid is Ruby Blossom.*

*Note the variation between
the flowers and the richly
colored lips on this example
of Ruby Blossom.*

**GROWING
DENDROBIUMS**

Seasonal activity
Plants grow in spring and
summer. They flower in spring
and rest in winter. Semi-
deciduous in cultivation.

Location
Greenhouse or sunroom.

Temperature
Summer maximum: 85°F(30°C)
Winter day: 60°F(16°C)
Night minimum: 50°F(10°C)

Light/Shade
Provide good light.

Watering/Spraying
Water well in summer, keep dry
in winter. Spray in spring
and summer.

Feeding
Spring, summer and fall.

*Sao Paulo is another
example of the breeding
from D.* nobile. *It needs
the same conditions.*

135

Lycastes, Calanthes & Angraecums

Lycastes are a group of strong-growing orchids originating from South America. They are allied to anguloas and can be hybridized to produce the genus *Angulocaste*. They have large, cone-shaped pseudobulbs, with several wide, broadly oval, ribbed leaves that are soft in texture and are shed after one season. These orchids remain deciduous in winter. All have distinctive three-cornered flowers formed by the flattened sepals; the inward-held petals and lip are smaller. In spring, the many stems carry single flowers in a range of colors, from white, through pinks and yellows to greens and reds. Grow cool, in good light and do not spray the leaves. Allow plenty of room to grow while in summer leaf. They are best suited to a greenhouse or sunroom.

Calanthes can be tried in a warm greenhouse. They produce large silvery green pseudobulbs topped with broadly oval, shortlived leaves in summer. While resting, the leafless pseudobulbs produce a flower spike in fall that can grow to 24in(60cm), with a cascade of wonderfully soft blooms, each one 2in(5cm)

Below: Anguloa clowesii, a wonderfully perfumed, summer-flowering species from Ecuador. The plant produces lush, seasonal foliage, becoming deciduous in the winter.

The other name for this plant is the cradle orchid, *which refers to the loosely hinged lip that can be rocked back and forth inside the cupped flower.*

Anguloa clowesii *is popularly known as the tulip orchid.*

Left: Calanthe vestita *and its hybrids produce flowers in winter from the leafless pseudobulbs. Colors range from white, through pink and light red to deep cerise.*

GROWING LYCASTES

Seasonal activity
Plants grow in spring and summer. They flower in spring and rest in winter. Deciduous.

Location
Greenhouse or sunroom with space for summer growth.

Temperature
Summer maximum: 80°F(27°C)
Winter day: 60°F(16°C)
Night minimum: 50°F(10°C)

Light/Shade
Provide good light.

Watering/Spraying
Water in spring, summer and fall. Do not spray leaves.

Feeding
Spring to fall.

Above: Lycaste aromatica *is a small-flowered, highly fragrant variety. It blooms in profusion in the spring as the new growth starts.*

Above: Angraecum sesquipedale, *the magnificent Star of Bethlehem orchid, produces its ivory-white blooms in winter. The flowers have long spurs.*

long and colored white, pink or red with a contrasting lip. The blooms will last for many weeks over the winter and spring. The best plants to grow are hybrids produced from the deciduous Old World species *Calanthe vestita*. These like a minimum temperature of 65°F(18°C) at night. They have a short, fast growing season, when you should keep them well watered and fed, but in shade. Annual repotting suits them. Do this in early spring, when new growths are just showing.

Angraecums are epiphytic orchids suitable for a warm greenhouse or sunroom kept at 65°F(18°C) as a winter night minimum. They enjoy moist, shady conditions and plenty of growing space, since they can grow to 24in(60cm) or more. There is a small choice of species and hybrids, including *Angraecum sesquipedale* from Madagascar or its hybrid *A. Veitchii*. Angraecums found in cultivation are large-growing plants, with pairs of leaves on a central, upwardly growing rhizome. In winter, several large, white waxy flowers, each with a long spur, are produced on a long spike.

GROWING ANGRAECUMS

Seasonal activity
Plants grow all year; slower in winter. They flower in winter. Evergreen.

Location
Greenhouse or sunroom.

Temperature
Summer maximum: 85°F(30°C)
Winter day: 75°F(24°C)
Night minimum: 65°F(18°C)

Light/Shade
Provide shade in summer.

Watering/Spraying
Water all year, less in winter. Spray lightly in summer.

Feeding
Spring to fall.

GROWING CALANTHES

Seasonal activity
Plants grow in spring and summer. They flower in winter and spring, and rest in winter. Deciduous.

Location
Warm greenhouse.

Temperature
Summer maximum: 85°F(30°C)
Winter day: 75°F(24°C)
Night minimum: 65°F(18°C)

Light/Shade
Shade in summer.

Watering/Spraying
Keep well watered in summer. Do not spray.

Feeding
Spring to fall.

Growing orchids indoors

Growing a selection of orchids indoors is undoubtedly the most straightforward and least demanding method of cultivation. Orchids will adjust to habitats not specially created for them and often grow extremely well and require the minimum of attention in a less than ideal environment. Indoors, the orchids are living with you and you spend much more time close to them, meeting their needs on a regular, even hourly basis! Try growing a small mixed collection on gravel-filled humidity trays. Net curtains at the window will protect them from the direct sun, and closing heavier curtains up against the glass on winter nights will ensure that cold does not damage nearby plants. If you prefer, you could grow a few orchids in a purpose-built growing case, which can provide a permanent home for a number of the smaller-growing varieties. The case can be automated with a small fan for air circulation and a humidity tray to help maintain some moisture around the plants. Bear in mind that orchids in pots indoors will dry out relatively quickly and will need frequent watering to keep them moist. Although spraying is not practical, sponge the leaves daily to keep them fresh and free from dust. Remember, a lone plant placed on a bright window with neither shade nor moisture and no other foliage around it is unlikely to succeed. Generally speaking, those orchids that do best indoors are those that need less light, particularly the hybrids. Try phalaenopsis and paphiopedilums in a warm room, and miltoniopsis, vuylstekearas and wilsonaras –along with other genera in the complex odontoglossum group – in cooler areas. The masdevallias will thrive in average temperatures when kept away from bright light.

Above: The basic essentials that you need for growing orchids indoors are a humidity tray filled with expanded clay pellets or gravel kept topped up with water. This will provide some moisture to rise around the plants in an otherwise dry environment.

Right: This type of arrangement can be used and improved upon to create a living display area featuring a variety of orchids growing with ferns and other foliage plants. The size and number of plants is only limited by the space you have available and the overall conditions. The plants relate to each other and provide themselves with their own growing environment.

Growing orchids in an aquarium

If you choose to grow some of the very tiny orchids, you may encounter problems due to their small stature. Small pots dry out within hours and the more immediate demands of these diminutive plants can be overlooked in a mixed collection. Ideally, miniature orchids need their own 'mini-micro' climate. A group of them in a finely controlled environment will succeed better than one or two lone plants competing alongside their larger relatives. An ideal solution is to grow and display them in an all-glass fish tank. Once inside their aquarium, the tiny orchids can remain permanently in position, either in a greenhouse, sunroom or indoors. In a room setting, the aquarium should be pleasing to the eye and can include a lid with tube lighting to enhance the display, as well as adding warmth. To maintain an attractive arrangement indoors, you can also include orchids of a suitable size while in bloom and return them to their normal growing area after flowering. Some orchids suitable for this type of culture would include the smaller species among the *Pleurothallis* and related groups. Many of these produce attractive plants with minute flowers, often blooming over a long period. There are also miniatures among the masdevallias and dryadellas that make ideal subjects for growing within the confines of an aquarium.

1 *Your aquarium will need a moisture base to maintain the level of humidity. Fill it to a depth of about 1in(2.5cm) using expanded clay pellets, pebbles or a similar material.*

2 *Provide a background to show off the orchids and other plants in the aquarium. Cork bark has a natural appearance and you can mount small plants directly onto it.*

3 *You can incorporate a few miniature tillandsias (bromeliads) to lend variety and interest to the display. You can easily attach these to the cork bark with staples.*

4 *Try placing the orchids in various positions in the tank until they look their best. Position the taller plants at the back, with the smallest species at the front. Be creative!*

This Miltoniopsis *can be shown off in the tank while in bloom, but is normally too large to grow here.*

Indoors, a lid fitted with tube lighting is useful in winter. Keep the lid open a little to avoid condensation.

Coelogyne ochracea *will eventually become too large for the tank, but can be displayed while it remains in bloom.*

ORCHIDS AND OTHER PLANTS FOR DISPLAY IN AN AQUARIUM

Orchids
Dryadella edwallii
Dryadella zebrina
Epidendrum polybulbon
Epidendrum porpax
Masdevallia chontalensis
Maxillaria tenuifolia
Pleurothallis aribuliodes
Pleurothallis grobyi
Promeneae citrina
Sigmatostalix radicans
Sophronitis coccinea

Other plants
Selaginella species
(Tree club moss)
Soleirolia soleirolii (Baby's tears)
Miniature *Tillandsia* species
(Bromeliads)

It should be possible to water the plants without removing them from the tank.

Keep the water level in the base to just below the stones. This will create humidity.

If too much water collects from watering, siphon some off. Do not allow plants to stand in water.

5 *It is a good idea to mist the interior of the aquarium regularly to keep up the level of humidity and to keep the plants fresh. A small plant sprayer is ideal for this purpose.*

141

Growing orchids in a sunroom

The sunroom is an area designed for relaxation and there are several good reasons for growing orchids here. To begin with, the central heating system can be taken directly from the house and run at very little extra cost. Secondly, the more time you spend among the orchids the better you can care for them, quickly spotting any problems and dealing with them as they arise. And finally, because this is a place to relax in, you will ensure that your sunroom is comfortable – neither too hot nor too cold – and these conditions will also suit the orchids. Place staging around the sides of the sunroom and install a system that will hold moisture under the plants. If you have a tiled floor, any water sprayed or spilled can be left to dry naturally without causing damage. Use the central area for table and chairs, and a tall plant if there is space. Control temperatures by shading and ventilating, and install tailor-made curtains or window shades that can be lowered to keep out the direct sun and to keep in warmth on winter nights. You can grow a wide range of orchids in a sunroom, but it may not be easy to create different temperature zones, so choose either all cool varieties or intermediate and warm ones. If you have plenty of headroom, try a few large specimen plants, such as cymbidiums or *Epidendrum ibaguense*.

Left: *Provide a staging that can accommodate the orchids, with a moisture stage underneath. This purpose-built slatted staging allows the moisture from a water-soaked gravel bed to rise around the plants.*

Right: *A sunroom furnished with phalaenopsis, cattleyas, miltoniopsis and dendrobiums. The roof is shaded outside with green emulsion paint and ornamental blinds can be lowered to protect plants against direct sun.*

Points to look out for when buying orchids

If you have never grown orchids before, you may be uncertain of what to buy and where to find stock. Most orchids are sold by specialist orchid nurseries, and it is a good idea to visit one of these to discover the range of orchids available and seek expert advice at the same time. Garden centers and some florists stock a few of the most popular orchids from time to time, but are often limited in the advice they can offer. If you cannot be sure of the conditions required by a plant, you are unlikely to succeed with it. Orchids are available either as young plants, needing several years to bloom, as first-time flowering plants or as large, mature specimens in full bloom. The price will vary according to the age and quality of the plant. Many of the orchid societies formed by enthusiastic amateur growers hold regular plant sales at their meetings and these can be the source of a good bargain. Wherever you obtain your orchids, look for healthy plants that are not in need of immediate repotting. It should not be necessary to check for pests, but aphids occasionally occur even in the best-run establishments. Check that foliage is clean and free from virus. If the plant is in bloom, ensure that the blooms are fresh, so that they will last for many weeks.

Below: Whether you buy plants in flower or a single cut bloom, make sure that the flowers are fresh enough to last for several weeks.

A fresh bloom with strong texture to the sepals and petals.

An old bloom showing a reddened lip with loss of texture.

A two-year-old seedling, one year out of the flask. It will be two or three years before it flowers.

This is a three-year-old plant, with still another year or two of growing to do before it flowers.

A young, flowering-size plant. When in season, plants of this size are available in bud.

Right: *For best results, try to buy established plants in pots, growing in a recommended potting mix. The prices of these miltoniopsis, for example, will vary according to the size of the plants. Always buy the best plants that you can afford.*

Left: *Commercially grown orchids are sown in sterile flasks. If you see them offered for sale, make sure that the plants are a good dark green and ready to be potted. Plants of this age are difficult for a beginner to handle and may not offer much variety.*

For instant results, look for a mature plant such as this, flowering at its full potential. It will cost more, but provides immediate enjoyment.

Sour-looking potting mix indicates overwatering.

Small pseudobulbs are an indication that there has been no progression in their growth.

Above: *A poor-looking specimen. This is a sick plant needing specialist care if it is to regain its health. It will be several years before it blooms.*

Below: *When this orchid is removed from its pot, you can see that it has made no roots because the bark has become sour. Do not buy such plants.*

145

Potting mixtures

Most orchids in cultivation are epiphytes that need open, well-drained potting mix. The most popular growing medium is non-resinous tree bark. Bark chippings come in different grades for large and small plants, are easy to handle and almost impossible to overwater. Peat is another organic mix, but it holds far more water and can become waterlogged. If it is left dry for long periods while orchids are resting, the acidity of the peat can change when it is watered again, causing roots to die. At one time, osmunda fiber was the basic potting material for all orchids. Today, it is expensive and difficult to obtain, but very useful for growing orchids on cork bark. Some commercially grown orchids are potted in an inert material, such as rockwool, which provides the plant with a moisture base, but you must add all the chemical nutrients and follow a precise feeding formula. If this causes a problem then transfer the plant to an organic potting mix.

This plant will take a few years to recover if repotted now.

Right: This Brassia verrucosa has not been repotted for many years and new growths have become increasingly weak. There are stunted roots outside the pot and signs of premature leaf loss on older pseudobulbs. The foliage is paler than normal.

Orchids root quickly and easily into bark potting mix. It decomposes slowly, releasing nutrients that provide most of the orchid's requirements. A little extra artificial feed helps to keep plants healthy.

A young plant potted in a fine grade of bark can be 'dropped on' every six months for successive years while the bark remains 'sweet' and in good condition. Chunks of bark provide space for air around the roots. Styrofoam pieces ensure swift drainage.

Peat-based potting mixes can also be used for most terrestrial and semi-terrestrial orchids. These are usually grown in half pots.

Below: *A selection of basic equipment for orchid growing. You can use a variety of containers, with styrofoam for crocking. Plastic pots are available in all sizes. Open, plastic pots for water plants are ideal for suspending the smaller species with roots that grow outside. Plastic hanging baskets accommodate the larger species and are easier to find than the wooden slatted baskets, although these are simple to make yourself. Cork bark is ideal for upward-growing orchids. You will need secateurs and wire to secure a plant onto cork, and bamboo canes, string, labels, pen, leaf wipes and a pruning knife. Keep methylated spirits, a toothbrush and scissors to hand for pest control. Colored labels help you to code your orchids, e.g. red to rest, blue to water, etc. This system is particularly useful in the winter.*

Rockwool and styrofoam granules provide an inorganic potting mix for this plant. As they have no food value, you must supply all the nutrients. The soft, open mix encourages quick root growth. Do not pack the rockwool too firmly and, ideally, wear a face mask to filter out any dry fibers in the air.

A potting mix made up of Finnish peat. Foam rubber pieces and styrofoam are added as aggregates to give more space and to aid swift drainage when watering.

147

Watering, spraying & feeding

Orchids need watering and spraying throughout their growing period. Some grow all year round, while others rest in winter. Plants often bloom while resting. Resting orchids require just enough water to keep the pseudobulbs from shriveling. A plant is resting between the formation of its last pseudobulb and the appearance of the next new growth, which may take a few weeks or several months. Orchids with short resting periods should be watered all year; do not let them dry out.

Spraying is another way of providing moisture, but does not take the place of watering. Daily spraying during spring and summer helps to cool the foliage during hot weather, deters pests and maintains humidity around the plants. Water and spray in the early part of the day when the temperature is rising. The leaves should be dry by the time the temperature starts to drop towards nightfall. Avoid spraying buds and flowers. Orchids will benefit from a light feed during their growing season. Those that grow all year round need less feed in winter and more in summer. You can apply the feed directly to the roots or spray it over the foliage. Use a specially formulated orchid feed according to the maker's instructions. As a general rule, feed the orchids at every second or third watering. The clear water will wash out any residue and prevents potentially harmful overfeeding.

Orchid feed is available in powder, granular or liquid form. If you use a general plant feed, mix it to the weakest recommended concentration.

Above: For orchids in bark, light feeding will supplement natural nutrients. In rockwool, an inert growing medium, regular feeding is important.

Below: Use a spouted watering can to flood the surface, giving the plant plenty of water at one application. Most of it will run through the potting mixture.

Below: *If a plant has become too dry, place it in a bowl of water and leave it to soak for up to one hour. You may need to hold it down for a while.*

Right: *In tropical rainforests, many orchids grow on trees and are drenched with rain each day. In a greenhouse, you can use a spray lance to imitate this effect.*

When spraying the foliage, avoid getting water onto the flowers, which can cause damp spots to appear.

Keep the water slightly below the base of the plant so that it does not get into the new growths and to prevent loose potting mixture from floating away.

Below: *Indoors, you must spray with more care. Use a hand-held spray bottle to mist the plant with water or a feed.*

Common growing problems

Common growing problems are the result of incorrect culture, which cause the orchid to show one or more signs of stress. Most problems are caused by extremes of heat and dryness that can build up in a greenhouse in summer or cold and wet in winter. Orchids with an overall yellowing of their foliage are suffering either from too much light or insufficient feeding. Increase the shading over them and use a nitrogen-based feed. The loss of the occasional leaf from the oldest pseudobulbs is natural, but a premature loss of leaves can be caused either by poisoning from fuel-burning heater fumes, root loss or extremes of heat or cold. Repot the plants as soon as possible, cutting out dead roots and old pseudobulbs. Shriveled pseudobulbs or limp foliage may be the result of under- or overwatering. Pseudobulbs become shriveled from lack of moisture and if roots are lost through overwatering, the result is the same. Given increased moisture, the underwatered plant will plump up again within weeks, but overwatered plants should be repotted and may take one or two years to recover. Dehydration of the foliage is also the result of incorrect watering; spraying the leaves helps prevent further moisture loss. Black tips or spotting on leaves are more often associated with low temperatures. It is false economy to grow orchids below the recommended minimum temperature, as this encourages fungal infections and problems with rotting.

Spray dehydrated leaves more often to help them regain their natural texture.

Shriveled pseudobulbs will plump up again when new roots appear from the young growth.

1 *An example of die back on a cattleya leaf caused by cold conditions. Cut off the affected part using a sharp, sterilized knife.*

2 *Using a cotton bud or paintbrush, carefully dust the cut with yellow sulfur to dry up the wound. Keep the affected area dry for a few days.*

Use yellow sulfur for all types of plant wounds.

Below: *Pseudobulbs should be plump at all times. Shriveling will result from under- or overwatering, or after repotting before new roots appear. Pseudobulbs may also become shriveled for a short time after a period of heavy flowering.*

Glossy, firm-textured leaves shine with good health.

Plump pseudobulbs will ensure an increase in the size of the next season's growth.

This plant has been overwatered and shows signs of premature leaf loss and leaf die-back. It will have no live roots.

A healthy plant should look like this. There is glossy, green foliage on all the pseudobulbs and their size increases each year. There are live roots in the pot.

Above: *Two cymbidiums - a healthy plant on the right and a weakened plant with growing problems on the left. The dying plant is unlikely to recover at this stage. Sadly, there is little alternative but to discard it.*

Right: *Exposure to direct sun will very quickly burn orchid leaves. This can easily happen in early spring before the greenhouse shading has been put in place. Placing sheets of newspaper over the plants will protect them until the shading is in position.*

1 Cut any black tips off leaves to prevent the die back from continuing to run back down the leaf. Use sterilized gardening tools.

2 Rather than cutting them square, trim leaf ends at an angle. This makes them look more natural and improves the appearance of the orchid.

If this Coelogyne has further spare 'eyes' at the base of the pseudobulbs, it means that more new growth will appear.

Left: Premature ageing or spotting of flowers can be the result of too much light or, as shown here, of water being sprayed directly onto the flowers. Low temperatures will have a similar effect.

If water collects in the top or hollow part of young growths, it will cause them to rot and eventually die.

Plump pseudobulbs, glossy foliage, strong new growth and a flower spike are all signs of a healthy plant.

Left: To save a plant in this condition, separate each pseudobulb and treat them as propagations. Where there are dormant 'eyes', they will grow.

152

Below: Two potted vuylstekearas. The one on the left is a healthy, growing, flowering plant, while the one on the right is ailing. Note the difference in condition of pseudobulbs and foliage.

Signs of neglect are corrugations on leaves, dryness in the early stage of growth, shriveled pseudobulbs and new growth dying back.

Below: Bud drop is a common condition caused by a sudden change in growing conditions. The buds turn yellow and drop off.

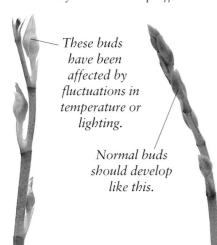

These buds have been affected by fluctuations in temperature or lighting.

Normal buds should develop like this.

1 *Basal rot has spread from a black, warty depression on the pseudobulb. Remove the pseudobulb by severing the rhizome to prevent rot from spreading.*

2 *The severed pseudobulb has a healthy, white rhizome at the base. A brown or black rhizome would indicate that the rot had spread further.*

A large depression has shrunk one side of this pseudobulb, causing it to become deformed.

Another dried-up blister is visible here. Cut the blister to release the liquid. Dry and pack the wound with sulfur.

3 *Keep a careful watch on a plant such as this in case basal rot reappears in another pseudobulb. They are all affected by black depressions - originally water-filled blisters - caused by cold and damp conditions.*

Basal rot affects some of the Oncidium species. This plant is O. leucochilum.

153

Keeping plants looking good

Taking a pride in the general appearance of your orchids is important if plants are to look good all year round. It also ensures that you quickly spot any pests that appear and can deal with them promptly. Greenhouse plants need an annual overhaul, say at repotting time. Remove dead back bulbs and any dead leaves that occur naturally from time to time. Do not allow leaves to decay on the bench, which encourages pests. In the home or sunroom, discreet ties can support broken or bending leaves, and split canes usually improve the angle of developing flower spikes. You can also use canes to control unmanageable pseudobulbs on cattleyas and dendrobiums, which may otherwise become top heavy, causing damage if they fall. Many orchids produce a protective sheathing that covers the young pseudobulbs and flower spikes as they progress. Once fully developed, the plant sheds this sheath, which turns brown. At this stage you can remove the sheaths from pseudobulbs to encourage end-of-season ripening, and from flower stems to prevent pests from harboring there.

Above: *Remove yellow leaves when they are 'ripe' enough to be picked easily from the plant. This is safer than cutting, which can spread virus disease when tools are used on another plant.*

Above: *Use leaf wipes or clean water to sponge foliage that has become dulled with hard water or residue from insecticides. It should not be necessary to use leaf shine on orchids.*

There is a clear line on the green leaf showing where it will eventually come away from the bract above the pseudobulb.

Remove dried bracts by splitting one at a time down each side of the pseudobulb and pulling away.

1 Cymbidium pseudobulbs that have shed their leaves are left with sharp, spiny bracts at the base. These look unsightly and can harbor pests, so remove them as shown here.

2 If you remove the bracts at the right stage, it will be quite easy for you to pull them away without causing any injury to the pseudobulbs.

Some of these back bulbs are surplus to the plant's requirements. The three in the foreground can be removed for propagation.

3 Once the back bulbs have been stripped of their bracts, they not only look better but will also receive more light to speed up ripening.

1 Cymbidium leaves are long-lived and can become damaged, spoiling the general look of the plant. Instead of cutting the leaves off, you can easily repair them using green string. In time, the string can be removed and the leaves will support themselves.

2 Use the undamaged center leaves to hold the outside leaves in place. Place the string around the center leaves and tie a knot.

The center leaves are strong enough to provide a support for the damaged leaves.

3 *Bring each leaf in turn towards the string tie and wrap the string around the leaf to hold it in position. Alternatively, use pieces of raffia.*

4 *Twist the string in between each leaf. There is no need to tie a knot behind every leaf; it will only make the string difficult to remove later on.*

5 *Finally, tie a knot behind the last leaf and cut off any surplus string. The finished repair can stay in place as long as the leaves remain on the plant.*

6 *Within a few months, you can carefully remove the string or raffia and the repaired leaves will once again be able to support themselves.*

Basic potting methods – dropping on

Dropping on is the easiest method of repotting an orchid. It simply involves taking a plant from its outgrown pot and placing it in a larger one without disturbing the root ball. It causes the minimum of disruption to the plant and can therefore be done at almost any time of the year. It is a good way for beginners to practice the potting technique and gain confidence before tackling the other methods featured on pages 160-163. Dropping on is ideal for young plants, and also for larger ones that are not ready for division. Orchids can be dropped on repeatedly for a number of years until the potting mix becomes completely decomposed and useless. It is important to use a potting mixture that matches the one in which the plant is already growing. Combining two mixes in one pot can lead to watering problems later on, as one type may be more porous and therefore need less water than the other.

A plant can be dropped on provided that it is healthy and growing well, with the majority of its pseudobulbs in leaf. It may need repotting because it has outgrown its pot or used up most of the food supply. When you remove the plant you should have a strong root system with live roots distributed evenly throughout the potting mix, binding it into a solid ball. The potting mix should be in good condition, not totally decomposed, and if containing bark, it should have a pleasant damp, woody aroma. Before dropping on, allow your plant to partially dry out. You can water it within a day or two of potting.

1 Ease the plant from the pot by squeezing it until the plant becomes loose and lifts out. Otherwise, cut the pot away. Notice the healthy roots here.

Styrofoam pieces are ideal for use as crocking.

2 Select a clean pot 2in(5cm) larger in diameter than the original one. Place just sufficient crocking material in the pot to cover the base. This will help to ensure good drainage.

Hold the plant steady with one hand and pour handfuls of potting mixture into the pot with the other. This bark has been dampened before use.

Make sure that the base of the plant is slightly below, and not above, the rim of the pot.

Add more potting mixture until the pot is full, not forgetting the sides.

3 Position your plant carefully in the new pot, leaving room at the front for it to grow forward. To do this, place the oldest pseudobulbs against one side of the pot.

Plastic pots are more popular than clay ones, because they are lighter, easier to use and non-porous.

4 Firm the potting mix by pressing it with your fingers around the rim of the pot, pushing it well down all round.

5 If the potting has been firmed, you should be able to lift the plant as shown here without the pot falling off. If this test fails, firm the potting mixture again using more pressure.

6 Firm potting is essential if the plant is to continue growing well for the next two years. Finally, do remember to replace the label; at this stage, many plants look alike!

Basic potting methods – repotting

The method of repotting a cymbidium featured here shows the standard procedure that can be followed for most orchids. Ideally, carry this out during the spring when the new growths are up to about 4in(10cm) long and before they have started to make their new roots. Repotting at the right stage of growth and at the ideal time of the year enables the plant to make a swift recovery with the minimum interruption to its growing cycle.

Repotting is an opportunity to clean out all the old, decomposed and exhausted potting mixture from under the plant. It also allows you to remove any old roots that have died naturally and any surplus back bulbs. You can often save the back bulbs and use them to propagate a further plant. Plants that have become too large can be divided where appropriate. You can split plants where sections with at least four pseudobulbs and a new growth can be kept as intact pieces. All or most of these pseudobulbs should be active and in leaf. If they are dormant, out-of-leaf back bulbs, divide them singly to encourage them to grow.

Repot plants while they are on the dry side. After repotting, do not water them for a few days to allow trimmed or broken roots time to heal and prevent any risk of rotting. But you can spray the foliage and potting mixture to prevent moisture loss during this period.

This is the back of the plant where the oldest (and smallest) pseudobulbs are. The plant will not produce new growth from here.

This is the new growth at the front of the plant. After repotting, this is where the new roots will come from.

The potting mix has largely broken down and has been replaced by the extensive roots. Note how thick and fleshy they are.

1 *The vigorous root system of this plant contains both living and dead roots. There are several pseudobulbs but the plant is not large enough to divide and there are no surplus back bulbs to remove.*

2 *Starting underneath, remove the crocks and all the old potting mix. Tease out the roots and shake the plant to release the mix. You may need to cut some roots to separate them.*

3 *Dead roots are dry and hollow. These are at the back and need to be cut away. Trim the live roots to a length of about 6in(15cm). If left long, these roots will snap and cause rotting.*

Place a handful or two of potting mixture on top of the crocking to bring the plant to the correct level in the pot. Fill in with potting mix while holding the plant steady.

4 *Using a new pot 2in(5cm) larger than the old one, position the plant with room in the front for new growth. Fold the roots underneath until the plant rests just below the pot rim.*

Basic potting methods – dividing

It is not always essential to divide orchids once they reach a certain size. If you prefer, you can grow them into specimen plants, with the majority of pseudobulbs in leaf. This is a good strategy with the smaller species, if they are to reach their full potential. However, the larger orchids, such as cymbidiums and cattleyas, can become unmanageable if allowed to reach their maximum size and may outgrow the space allocated to them. A good time to divide a plant is when it has grown in two or more directions at the same time and its irregular shape will not allow it to fit easily into a larger pot. A new pot would have to be so large that the result would be overpotting, and overwatering would become unavoidable. Sometimes, the middle of a plant contains a surplus of leafless back bulbs. Remove these to prevent them from becoming a strain on the plant. Cutting away such unwanted back bulbs is an easy way of dividing the plant into pieces. Do make sure that each piece has at least four pseudobulbs on it; very small divisions will reduce the plant's flowering ability until it has regained its vigor, which could take two or three years. Dividing has several advantages. Not only do you reduce the size of the plant, but you also increase your stock and create 'spare' plants to exchange with fellow enthusiasts. Alternatively, you may prefer to keep the extra plants and try growing them in different positions. This is a useful tactic when a plant has been reluctant to bloom.

All these pseudobulbs are in leaf, with no surplus back bulbs to remove.

1 *This* Laelia autumnalis *has grown in two directions. Repotting would mean overpotting it, unless you place it in an oblong basket. It is an ideal candidate for dividing.*

If the plant had been repotted before these new roots had grown, there would be no risk of damaging them as you divide the plant.

On this pseudobulb, this year's roots have not yet started to grow, which is an advantage.

2 *Out of its pot, you can see how orchids make roots in and out of the potting mixture. Aerial roots will not grow in potting mix; new underground ones will grow.*

Use a sharp knife to make a clean cut through the rhizome.

Take care to avoid slicing into the base of the fleshy pseudobulbs.

It is impossible to avoid damaging these young growing roots. New ones will appear soon after repotting.

It should be easy to pull apart the two halves. If necessary, cut through the roots.

3 As you divide the plant, leave a minimum of four pseudobulbs on each division to avoid reducing the flowering ability of the plant. Smaller divisions than this will take several years to reach flowering size. Separate the plant by cutting vertically through the rhizome joining the pseudobulbs, using a sharp knife sterilized by dipping it in methylated spirits.

Stand plants with their new growths facing forwards, so that you can observe their progress. Replace labels at the back.

4 Now you can pot up the two halves in suitably sized pots, as described on pages 160-161. Some shriveling may occur before new growths and roots appear. In the meantime, keep the potting mixture moist and spray well.

Part Six

HOUSEPLANT SELECTION

Houseplants are immensely rewarding to grow, responding to good care and attention almost like potted pets. Use them to brighten up rooms with living color or fresh green foliage. Team plants with ornamental containers such as baskets, pottery or gnarled chunks of driftwood to create stunning 'still life' displays all round the house. Use trailing plants in hanging containers to bring windows to life, and have fun creating imaginatively planted bowls, terrariums or bottle gardens. Grouping plants together in displays not only makes the most of their attractions, but also allows them to help each other thrive by creating a 'micro-climate' of moist air around them. Plants help condition the air, too; many kinds remove harmful pollutants as well as releasing water vapor and oxygen from their leaves. Each plant has its own personality; its size, shape and growth habit as well as individual preferences for growing conditions make it suitable for different rooms or situations. They are not difficult to look after, and rarely suffer from problems when correctly cared for. Far more are killed by excess kindness than neglect – overwatering or intermittent watering, when plants are alternately allowed to wilt then stood up to their necks in water for days, are by far the commonest causes of failure. A little basic advice is all it takes to start growing them succesfully. Enjoy getting to know houseplants, and the charm they can bring to your home. The following pages show a selection of popular houseplants that you may wish to add to your growing interior displays.

Left: Solenostemon *(Coleus) are colorful, easy-care houseplants.* ***Right:*** *The textured leaves of* Pilea *'Moon Valley'*

Achimenes 'Johanna Michelssen' (Hot water plant)

Aeschynanthus 'Mona Lisa' (Lipstick vine)

Aglaonema 'Maria' (Chinese evergreen)

Asparagus densiflorus 'Sprengeri' (Emerald fern)

Asparagus falcatus (Sicklethorn)

Asparagus setaceus (Asparagus fern)

Aspidistra elatior (Cast-iron plant)

Begonia masoniana (Iron cross begonia)

Begonia rex hybrids (King, painted leaf, fan begonia)

Calathea makoyana (Peacock plant)

Aglaonema 'Lillian'
(Chinese evergreen)

Anthurium andreanum
'Carré' (Tail flower)

Anthurium scherzerianum
(Flamingo flower)

Aphelandra squarrosa
'Louisae' (Zebra plant)

Begonia maculata
(Cane-stemmed begonia)

Pendulous begonia
(Begonia)

Begonia 'Elatior'
hybrid (Begonia)

Begonia boweri
'Tiger Paws' (Eyelash begonia)

Calathea zebrina
(Peacock plant, zebra plant)

Ctenanthe 'Golden Mosaic'
(Ctenanthe)

Stromanthe 'Stripestar'
(Stromanthe)

Chlorophytum comosum
'Variegatum' (Spider plant)

Cissus rhombifolia
(Grape ivy)

Cissus rhombifolia
'Ellen Danica' (Grape ivy)

Clivia miniata
(Clivia)

Cordyline fruticosa
'Kiwi' (Ti plant)

Cordyline fruticosa 'Lord
Robertson' (Ti plant)

Dieffenbachia 'Camilla'
(Dumb cane)

Dieffenbachia seguine
'Tropic Snow' (Dumb cane)

Dieffenbachia 'Veerle
Compacta' (Dumb cane)

Dracaena deremensis
'Green Stripe' (Dracaena)

Codiaeum 'Red Curl'
(Croton)

Codiaeum 'Goldstar'
(Croton)

Codiaeum 'Petra'
(Croton)

Columnea 'Wilde Brand'
(Goldfish plant)

Cordyline fruticosa 'Red Edge'
(Ti plant)

Cyclamen cultivar
(Cyclamen)

Cyperus albostriatus
(Umbrella plant)

Cyperus cyperoides
(Umbrella plant)

Dracaena fragrans
'Massangeana'
(Dracaena)

Epipremnum aureum
(Devil's ivy)

Epipremnum 'Marble Queen'
(Devil's ivy)

Epipremnum 'Neon'
(Devil's ivy)

Euphorbia pulcherrima
(Poinsettia)

Fatsia japonica
(Japanese aralia)

Ficus elastica 'Robusta'
(Rubber plant)

Ficus lyrata 'Audrey'
(Fiddle-leaf fig)

Hedera canariensis
'Montgomery' (Ivy)

Hedera helix 'Goldchild'
(Ivy)

170

x Fatshedera lizei 'Pia'
(Tree ivy)

Ficus benjamina 'De Gantel'
(Weeping fig)

Ficus benjamina (with plaited stems)
(Weeping fig)

Ficus elastica 'Tineke'
(Rubber plant)

Fittonia verschaffeltii var.
argyroneura 'Nana' (Mosaic plant)

Fittonia v. var. *pearcei*
'Superba Red' (Mosaic plant)

Gardenia augusta
(Cape jessamine)

Hedera algeriensis
'Gloire de Marengo' (Ivy)

Hedera helix 'Mini Heron'
(Ivy)

Hedera helix 'Pittsburgh'
(Ivy)

Hibiscus rosa-sinensis
'Paramaribo' (Rose of China)

Hoya carnosa 'Tricolor'
(Wax plant)

171

Hoya lanceolata spp. *bella*
(Miniature wax plant)

Hydrangea macrophylla
'Libelle' (Lacecap hydrangea)

Hydrangea macrophylla 'Bodensee'
(Hortensia hydrangea)

Jasminum officinale
(Common white jasmine)

Justicia brandegeeana
(Shrimp plant)

Kalanchoe blossfeldiana
(Flaming Katy)

Kalanchoe pumila
(Kalanchoe)

Maranta leuconeura var.
erythroneura (Herringbone plant)

Maranta leuconeura var.
kerchoveana (Rabbit's foot plant)

Monstera deliciosa
(Swiss cheese plant)

Nolina (Beaucarnea) recurvata
(Pony tail palm)

Hypoestes phyllostachya
(Polkadot plant)

Impatiens walleriana
(Busy Lizzie)

Kalanchoe 'Tessa'
(Kalanchoe)

Large-flowered and 'mini-zonal'
Pelargonium (Geranium)

Pelargonium graveolens
(Scented-leaf geranium)

Peperomia caperata 'Luna' (Emerald ripple
peperomia, pepper elder)

Peperomia obtusifolia 'Green Gold' (Pepper elder)

Philodendron erubescens 'Imperial Red' (Blushing philodendron)

Philodendron 'Medisa' (Philodendron)

Philodendron scandens (Sweetheart plant)

Radermachera sinica (Emerald tree)

Rhododendron 'Rosali' (Azalea)

Rhododendron (standard form) (Azalea)

Saintpaulia 'Ramona' (African violet)

Schefflera 'Amate' (Umbrella tree)

Schefflera arboricola 'Compacta' (Parasol plant)

Schefflera arboricola 'Trinette' (Parasol plant)

Sinningia cultivar (Gloxinia)

Pilea 'Moon Valley'
(Aluminum plant)

Pilea cadieri
(Aluminum plant)

Plectranthus coleoides 'Marginatus'
(Candle plant)

Sansevieria trifasciata
(Mother-in-law's tongue)

S. t. 'Laurentii'

S. t. 'Golden
Futura'

Saxifraga stolonifera
(Mother of thousands)

Saxifraga stolonifera
'Tricolor' (Mother of thousands)

S. t. 'Golden
Hahnii'

Solanum pseudocapsicum
(Jerusalem cherry)

*Capsicum annuum (related to
Solanum)* (Ornamental pepper)

175

Soleirolia soleirolii
'Aurea' (Baby's tears)

Solenostemon varieties
(Coleus, painted nettle)

Spathiphyllum 'Cupido'
(Peace lily)

Stephanotis floribunda
(Madagascar jasmine)

Streptocarpus 'Maassen's
White' (Cape primrose)

Syngonium 'Arrow'
(Goosefoot plant)

Tolmiea menziesii 'Taff's
Gold' (Piggyback plant)

Tradescantia varieties
(Inch plant, spiderwort)

Yucca elephantipes
(Yucca)

Spathiphyllum
'Sensation' (Peace lily)

Aechmea fasciata
(Urn plant)

Ananas comosus variegatus
(Variegated pineapple)

Syngonium 'Infrared'
(Goosefoot plant)

Cryptanthus bivittatus
(Earth star)

Guzmania 'Rana'
(Guzmania)

Yucca elephantipes 'Jewel'
(Yucca)

Neoregelia 'Tricolor
Perfecta' (Neoregelia)

Tillandsia
(Air plants)

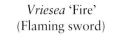

Vriesea 'Fire'
(Flaming sword)

INDOOR BULBS

Hippeastrum 'Minerva'
(Amaryllis)

DESERT CACTI

Cleistocactus strausii

Parodia scopa

Echinopsis chamaecereus

Mammillaria baumii

FOREST CACTI

Hyacinthus 'Blue Delft' (Hyacinth)

Epiphyllum 'Pegasus'
(Orchid cactus)

Schlumbergera hybrid
(Christmas cactus)

Adiantum bicolor
(Maidenhair fern)

Adiantum capillus-veneris
(Maidenhair fern)

Asplenium nidus
(Bird's nest fern)

Blechnum gibbum
(Dwarf tree fern)

Cyrtomium falcatum
(Holly fern)

Didymochlaena truncatula
(Cloak fern)

Dryopteris erythrosora
(Copper shield fern)

Nephrolepis exaltata 'Dallas Jewel' (Sword fern)

Pellaea rotundifolia
(Button fern)

Platycerium bifurcatur
(Staghorn fern)

Pteris cretica 'Albolineata'
(Brake fern)

Caryota mitis
(Fishtail palm)

Chamaedora elegans
(Parlor palm)

Chrysalidocarpus lutescens
(Areca palm)

Howea forsteriana
(Kentia palm)

Phoenix canariensis
(Canary Island date palm)

SUCCULENTS

Crassula ovata
(Jade plant)

Haworthia attenuata

Echeveria 'Perle von Nurnberg'

Echeveria 'Black Prince'

x *Pachyveria* hybrid

Browallia speciosa
(Amethyst flower)

Catharanthus roseus
(Madagascar periwinkle)

Dendranthema x
grandiflorum
(Pot chrysanthemum)

Eustoma grandiflorum
(Prairie gentian)

Exacum affine
(Arabian violet)

Gerbera jamesonii
(Barbeton daisy)

Senecio cruentus
(Cineraria)

Primula obconica
(Primrose)

Index to Plants

Page numbers in **bold** indicate major text references. Page numbers in *italics* indicate captions and annotations to photographs. Other text entries are shown in normal type.

Credits

The majority of the photographs featured in this book have been taken by Neil Sutherland and are © Quadrillion Publishing. The publishers wish to thank the following photographers for providing additional photographs, credited here by page number and position on the page, i.e. (B)Bottom, (T)Top, (C)Center, (BL)Bottom left, etc.

Gillian Beckett: 69(TC)
Eric Crichton: 69(L), 72(TR), 75(TC), 136(BL), 137(TR)
Garden Matters/John Feltwell: 71(R)
Garden Picture Library/Steven Wooster: 69(BR)
John Glover: 68(T), 73(TL), 79(TC)
Clive Nichols: 76(T)
Photos Horticultural: 68(B), 70(T,B)
Elizabeth Whiting Associates: 71(L)

Acknowledgements

The publishers would like to thank the following people and organizations for their help: Barnsfold Nurseries, Tismans Common, Sussex; Chessington Nurseries; Burnham Nurseries, Newton Abbott, Devon; China's Bonsai; Clarke & Spiers, Ripley, Surrey; The Flower Auction Holland, Naaldwijk, The Netherlands; Forest Lodge Garden Center, Farnham, Surrey; Herons Nursery; Hollygate Cactus Nursery, Ashington, Sussex; Secretts Garden Center, Milford, Surrey; Iden Croft Herbs, Staplehurst, Kent; Bill Jordan; Allan Smith Nurseries, Titchfield, Hants.; Philip Sonneville nv, Lochristi, Belgium; Ruth Stafford-Jones; Vesutor Air Plants, Billingshurst, Sussex.